Women's Liberation in China

MARXIST THEORY AND CONTEMPORARY CAPITALISM

General Editor: John Mepham
This is a new series of texts, of new British books and of translations, committed to:
the development of Marxist theory
the analysis of contemporary capitalism, its tendencies and contradictions
the record of struggles to which they give rise.

Also in this series:

Charles Bettelheim
The Transition to Socialist Economy

Michel Bosquet
Capitalism in Crisis and Everyday Life

Lucien Sève
Man in Marxist Theory and the Psychology of Personality

Colin Henfrey and Bernardo Sorj (eds.)
Chilean Voices: Activists Describe their Experiences of the Popular Unity Period

Women's Liberation in China

Claudie Broyelle

with a Preface by
Han Suyin

Translated from the French by
Michèle Cohen and Gary Herman

Humanities Press

First published in USA in 1977 by
Humanities Press Inc.,
Atlantic Highlands, NJ 07716

© 1977 Harvester Press Ltd

Library of Congress Cataloging in Publication Data

Broyelle, Claudie.
    Women's liberation in China.

    (Marxist theory and contemporary capitalism)
    Translation of La moitié du ciel.
    Includes bibliographical references
    1. Women – China. 2. Feminism – China.
    3. China – Social conditions. I. Title II. Series
    HQ1738.B7613   301.41'2'0951   76-4524
    ISBN 0-391-00587-1

First published in France as
La Moitié du Ciel
by Editions Denoël/Gonthier, 1973

Translated from the French by
Michèle Cohen and Gary Herman

Printed in England by
Redwood Burn Ltd., Wiltshire

All rights reserved

Contents

Preface by Han Suyin	vii
Translators' note	ix
Introduction	x
Foreword to the English edition	xi
A fivefold reality	3

Part One   Work is changing women; women are changing work

Introduction	9
1 The Chinese road to industrialization and women's liberation	11
2 The socialization of the Chinese countryside and women's liberation	25

Part Two   Socializing housework

Introduction	35
3 Collectivization first, then mechanization	40
4 The example of Taching	49
5 Domestic production demystified	57

Part Three   Socializing the mother's function

6 Infancy and early childhood	67
7 Children are people	77
8 Child-rearing and education: the province of society or of the State?	97

Part Four   The Chinese family – towards a new grass-roots collectivity

Introduction	107
9 A historical survey	108
10 Leisure time, work time	118
11 The idea of 'nationalization' and its fatal consequences for the family	125

Part Five   A contribution to the debate on sexuality in China

Introduction	137
12 Natural needs and cultural needs	138
13 A new sexual culture is beginning in China	144
14 A new idea of love	150

In place of a conclusion	155
Appendix	156
Afterword: Against the eternal woman	158
Notes and references	159

HAN SUYIN
Preface

It makes me very happy to write a preface for this book, which I consider to be an excellent, thoughtful and necessary work in order to clear up the very confused thinking of many women, all over the western world, as regards themselves.

The Chinese experience, or rather the massive revolutionary experiment, in the continuing revolution of China, has indubitably and from the very beginning been linked with woman's true liberation, in every sense of the word. In fact it is impossible to conceive of a socialist revolution in China which would have taken in only 'half the population', and left the other half in the condition of servitude and exploitation which is still massively the lot of women all over the world. But the Chinese in this, as in so many other spheres of action, do not proceed with *a priori* ideas, with opportunism, or with any idea that woman's liberation goes through the gestures of merely 'giving them' legal equality, economic equality, and then not doing any more. It is the profound transformation of woman herself, in her own evaluation of self and the group, the revalorization of every so-called 'value' ascribed to woman's relations with society, with the family, with men, with their own function as mothers and wives as well as workers, which is described in detail, and which will be a revelation to many women who want their condition to change, but often get hold of the wrong way of doing it.

Far be it from me to look down on or to denigrate the women's liberation movements now occurring in many countries in the West; as Premier Chou En-lai said of the young, there are all manners of seeking for a way, for the truth; and all genuine movements begin with these gropings. But it is also necessary for all women who truly want liberation to study this book, because here the struggle of women in China on the ideological and material planes, not only to transform society and 'make the revolution' but also to transform themselves, is expressed with great clarity. Everywhere there are anecdotes, vivid life stories, to illustrate the points made. And the great leap forward of Chinese women is best seen in the fact that they are not liberating themselves *only* in order to attain equality with men and economic benefits, but in order to 'make the revolution', to contribute to the consolidation of socialism, for only in this consolidation can they also consolidate their own liberation, and truly become 'half of heaven'.

I confess that in reading this book I found that I myself was deficient in a good many ways in my understanding of women, that I too still harboured some 'feudal' and 'retrograde' ideas on women's condition. This is due to the fact that I am limited by my own experience. Mine has been an individual experience of struggle to attain the right to expression, and because of this very experience, I have tended to ignore many details of woman's servitude, having escaped them myself, and even forgotten how very eroding they are. This book has therefore taught me a good many things, and I congratulate the author with all my heart on having produced this work, which relates practice to theory, which gets away from paternalism, the self-satisfaction of thinking that 'the fight was won' and that once women were enjoying *improved status* there was nothing more to ask for.

Very often in my speeches in many western countries I encounter men and women who seem convinced that 'sexual relations' and 'liberation of sex', which means sex for women and young girls without the bond of marriage, is the absolute liberation. At any rate this is the impression they give, because they seem to rest all their hopes on this one aspect, thinking that once this is attained, everything else is of secondary interest. I have fought against this notion, for relations with men are a function of the social aspect. But I see now that I did not have enough understanding of how truly pernicious this 'sex theory' is. The chapter "A contribution to the debate on sexuality in China" is a piece of work which I found of great importance to illuminate this subject.

I hope that all women, and many men too, will read this book. Perhaps in some cases (with reference to domestic work, for instance, where the authors seem to feel that men as well as women must participate fully) the point made may shock some men. But it is good to remind them to what extent women's energy goes into the daily chores of housework, which even the best of men consider to be the province of women. It is good to rethink this problem too, although the tendency to think in terms of 'family' (and inevitably, once one thinks of the 'aptitude' of women to be housewives and mothers the tendency to divide housework arbitrarily so that finally the whole burden of it falls on them) is very strong and will probably make this point very difficult to absorb. There will certainly always be a difference: for instance, men cannot go through the sufferings of childbirth. But surely the thing to do, as the author suggests, is to revalorize the importance and preciousness of woman's production – including the all-important one of giving birth – by placing it on the plane of socialist and proletarian values; and the same goes for housework. I am very grateful to the authors for their courage and the penetrating clarity with which they have dissected all these problems. Their excellent work will, I hope, make many more ideas germinate in all those women who are truly concerned with changing themselves and their social condition, and thereby the world.

Translators' Note

There is one thing which no translator can do without. That is the sympathy, knowledge and help of others more expert in particular areas. Our thanks must be given here to Noelle Gray, librarian at the Society for Anglo-Chinese Understanding, and Elisabeth Croll, of the School of Oriental and African Studies. Finally, our thanks go to our editor, to our long-suffering friends and, of course, to Claudie Broyelle.

MICHÈLE COHEN AND GARY HERMAN
London, 1975

Introduction

We visited China in November 1971. When I say we, I refer to twelve women from Paris and the French provinces. We were students and office workers, one peasant and a working-class grandmother. We included single women and mothers with anything from one to six children. But one thing we all had in common was that we were activists in the struggle for women's liberation.

However, this book should not be considered to be the unified view of our group; nor is it the product of a collective effort. I alone bear the responsibility for the opinions expressed herein, which may differ from those of my comrades.

I should like to thank Françoise Chomienne for her help in writing the book.

CLAUDIE BROYELLE

Foreword to the English Edition

I wrote this book following a journey made in November 1971. Today I should like to draw the attention of readers to two very important points.

Firstly, the book is not by any means a final account, still less an estimate of the average degree of women's emancipation in China. I have tried to outline orientations and trends. It is, if you like, a book about the 'Chinese road' toward the emancipation of women. The road itself is a winding one and often seems uncertain of its direction – but the route can be clearly seen and the overall direction discovered.

Secondly, the book is also, and perhaps just as much, about the problems we women in the West face in today's struggle for our own emancipation. I have always thought, and still do, that a study of the Chinese experience in this area is an absolutely vital prerequisite for any clarification of the arguments about 'women's liberation and social liberation'. Just as vital, in fact, as learning from the failure of the Russian Revolution, which I consider to be the greatest tragedy of the workers' (and therefore of the women's) movement. I am more than ever convinced that despite the undeniable and timely gains of the new women's movement, the most important thing is still to 'dismantle', as a watchmaker would a watch, the complex and precise mechanism of women's oppression – both the machinery supporting the specific situation of women and the organic network of its connections with the exploitative society. We can no longer be content with platitudes about women's condition or with received ideas (even if they do happen to be fashionable) about 'phallocracy'. The directions we must take on the journey towards our liberation are written in their entirety in the material base of our oppression – and I think that everything, or almost everything, is yet to be done.

I should like to add one more point. I often read (and hear) that socialism, 'even in China', doesn't liberate women. Where is the evidence for this observation? There are still fewer women than men in administrative positions, women still do more work than men in the home and more looking after children, and so on. But what these arguments ignore is that there is a sense in which socialism doesn't liberate the proletariat either, 'even in China'. The wage system still exists; there are still important divisions between manual workers and intellectuals and between urban and rural areas; there is still the State. There is still class and the class struggle. There is a constant danger of capitalism being restored. You have to be blind not to see this possibility. To me the real issues are altogether different. We must look at the existence of workers' power in a socialist society – that is, a society whose twin characteristics are the destruction of social relations of production based on exploitation (in China, both capitalist and feudal relations) and the embryonic emergence of new communist social relations – and we must ask if that is the sole condition to be fulfilled before the long march of women's liberation can get fully under way. And we must also ask whether or not workers' power is viable without the developing struggle of millions of women to break their age-old chains.

I should like the English edition to make some contribution towards the discussion of these issues.

As for the rest, the book contains some debatable arguments and a number of major or minor errors. I am aware of a few of these but not of others, and in any case I think it would be dishonest to correct them now. I originally wanted to submit raw material, warts and all, to be refined in discussion and debate about our cause. I still do. It is clear to me that this discussion and debate emphatically result in a demand that we should return to Marxism.

CLAUDIE BROYELLE
Peking, July 1974

WOMEN CARRY HALF OF HEAVEN ON
THEIR SHOULDERS AND THEY MUST
CONQUER IT
(MAO TSE-TUNG)

A Fivefold Reality

The very existence of the new women's movement poses a number of questions. The first one is: why is there a women's movement at all today? After all, women have the right to vote in all countries where the movement exists; so that wasn't the reason why they formed women's groups. We have the right to divorce, to a limited degree. A limited right to contraception has recently been achieved in France. Nowadays almost all women have experience, at some time in their lives, of social labour. The principle of 'equal pay for equal work' has even been written into the bourgeois code of work.

Recent reforms in the marriage laws have attenuated some of the more glaring instances of sexual discrimination. Today, universities are open to women. And, last of all, a large number of household appliances are widely available these days to lighten the burden of housework.

Then why have a women's movement? Historically, women have accomplished a great deal, and yet they find themselves virtually back at square one, still oppressed. We know that the right to work, to vote, to get divorced, to study, to use contraceptives and an electric coffee grinder haven't really freed us from domestic slavery, from compulsory motherhood or from economic dependence on our husbands, any more than our political rights have enabled us to change society in any way. This means that our oppression isn't rooted in the absence of these rights. In fact not only have these reforms not liberated us; they have made us feel our oppression even more cruelly.

'What do women want?' cries the panic-struck bourgeois legislator 'After all, we've given them everything!' Quite right! They have given us everything (or almost everything) – everything allowed under capitalism, that is.

And it's not much!

We can expect nothing from this society. The cycle had to be completed, and all the illusory hopes for legal solutions to our problems, which characterized the earlier women's movements, had to be thoroughly shattered before a new women's movement could appear. Even though the new movement isn't always aware of it, its existence and nature are determined by the experience and limitations of the earlier movement. Yet with this starting-point, everything remains to be done.

But if our lack of legal rights had nothing to do with our real oppression, what does it stem from? It is clearly important for anyone concerned for the future of women to discover the causes and to investigate the forms and consequences of women's oppression in order to develop a theory which can be used in attacking it. But this doesn't interest the French women's liberation movement very much. For them women's oppression is 'lived experience', to be 'felt' rather than explained. They believe that we live under the tyranny of non-communication. That no man can rise above himself sufficiently to understand the female condition. And that women who live their oppression have no need to analyse it, and even less need to build a theory about their liberation. In any case, they say, theories are made for men by men — that's male territory.

But many of us think we must go beyond this 'feminism'. It doesn't take much time to survey the true stories of women's oppression — the women's liberation movement has heaps of them. They contribute about as much to our cause as stories of factory life enlighten the proletariat about their tasks. We want to go further. In its infancy, the oppressed working class turned its anger against machines; later it built the Paris Commune. The distance between these two stages is the distance still to be covered between the revolt against 'the male' and the liberation of women.

Everything we saw in China confirms this, and what we learned helped us to clear up a misunderstanding: the emancipation of women cannot be a separate task, an 'extra bit of soul' that gives socialism a human face. Take sexuality for example: any attempt to free women from the myths of passivity and of woman as sex object is no more than wishful thinking if we don't apply ourselves equally to the task of destroying that economic dependence which is precisely what forces women to be passive and to play the role of object; that is, unless we also attack the economic and political functions of the bourgeois nuclear family in which women are trapped. The patriarchal family has its *raison d'être* in the capitalist system. Schools aren't the diabolical inventions of teachers any more than the family is the fruit of men's wickedness. Those who act in a play don't set the scenes. These institutions are machines, indispensable devices, enabling workers to go to work each day, and their children to learn day after day the role that society assigns to them.

This is the reason why capitalism, although always eager for novelty and transformation, preserves one of the most ancient cottage industries: the domestic workshop where 'honest workers' and their docile wives are trained and become conscious of their duties and respectful of other people's property. Capitalism must ensure that women, the skilled workers who provide this noble service, are not diverted from such profitable work, even when it has to use them as a pool of reserve labour. In either case, it is vital that they should continue to fulfil their domestic role.

You can't break a machine unless you know how it works. To be sure, domestic slavery and the mother's role are strengthened and morally sanctified by myths and illusions, but they are the very chains which bind a woman to the restricted network of her daily activities; it is precisely because women prepare vegetables and do the washing up that they see these chores as a talent, a vocation, a destiny. It is the material base that gives birth to the illusions and myths of feminity, and not vice versa.

A FIVEFOLD REALITY

Beyond all the talk about the 'essence' of womanhood the reality is that to be a woman under capitalism means to be involved in five main kinds of social relations, to have a particular relationship to:
- social labour
- housework
- children
- the family
- sexuality.

But these five aspects of oppression are not all equivalent and interchangeable. Thus it is no accident that the first chapter of this book deals with social production and is immediately followed by a chapter on housework: women are oppressed because of the division of labour in our society, which excludes them from social production and limits them to doing housework. That is why the first step towards the emancipation of women is to ensure that they are fully able to participate in social labour. Without that all the discussion about women's liberation is just empty words. And it is no accident either that sexuality comes last in this book: we must describe the framework within which it exists before trying to analyse how the question of sexuality is objectively raised in China today. Again, it's no accident that the chapter on children's liberation occupies the centre of the book, after the chapter on housework and its socialization and before that on the family. Motherhood can operate in capitalist society only if women are excluded from social labour, for that's where its original function lies. To understand the changes that have come about in China, from the point of view of women's liberation and the revolution in child-rearing and education, we first had to outline the new role that women are playing in different social activities. Conversely, any approach to the family in China would have been useless without a previous study not only of the new ties that bind women who belong to these families to society as a whole, but also of the new role that children are playing in society, and the way in which society takes upon itself the task of looking after them.

Because we are revolutionary women people see us as torn between our different aims: we are expected to say that as women we wish to struggle against men, while as revolutionaries we are struggling against capitalism.

But we're not 'torn' and we don't want to reconcile women and revolution like two hostile sisters. Our project is altogether different: we want to see and understand exactly how a revolutionary society, socialism, liberates women. We ask both what socialism will do for women, which is of obvious interest, and also, most emphatically, how the very existence and development of that socialist society necessitate the liberation of women. In other words, we want to know what the internal, dialectical connections are between women and revolution, the part and the whole.

'Women are one half of heaven,' says Mao, and if that part of heaven remains unmoved, the revolutionary storms which should sweep away the old world will turn out to be only passing showers.

With all this in mind we organized a trip to China to study the condition of women in Chinese society. More precisely, we wanted to chart the course of the Chinese revolution from the point of view of women's liberation in order to try to identify the effects of one on the other.

However, I must warn readers against too hasty an interpretation of this book. They will not find a 'stock taking' of the Chinese situation. We ourselves are too far away from such a comprehensive view even to think of *sketching* it. Each of the revolutionary positions we have tried to bring out, study and comment on is counterbalanced by a reactionary bourgeois position which tries to smother it. The revolution doesn't advance in a straight line. It can't be programmed, but follows an uneven course. So you mustn't take all the progressive experiments as indicative of the norm for the whole of China. We came across particularly exciting ones in some places, but found that they were almost unknown in others.

In Shaoshan, Mao Tse-tung's birthplace, the political commissar of the People's Liberation Army (PLA) in that region gave us an interview in which he told us: 'It is absolutely necessary to realize that China is not all red. For instance there are a handful of reactionaries supporters of American imperialism, in China today. If we lose sight of that reality, we will fail in all our plans. You, too, must absolutely not believe that all is well in China. You can't say that all is well in China, since there are still reactionaries, reactionary ideas and reactionary practices. Two things are fighting it out: on the one hand, the revolution; on the other, the counter-revolution. Of course it is through this struggle that socialism develops; but if we fail in this struggle, socialism will die. In other words, the question as to who – bourgeoisie or proletariat – will prevail in China still remains unanswered today.'

Part One
WORK IS CHANGING WOMEN; WOMEN ARE CHANGING WORK

Introduction

Immediately after its liberation in 1949, China was faced with the problem of how to involve in social production the many millions of women confined until then in narrow domesticity. China was in a good position to bring about this upheaval. In particular, the victory of the revolution, crowning twenty years of national and civil wars, had profoundly transformed the old society and had destroyed many of the old ideas about women's inferiority. Millions of women had played an active part in the war against the Japanese; they had exercised power directly, often playing a leading part in the liberated areas. In many districts they had frequently taken charge of agricultural production. This wealth of experience was the context in which the question of achieving emancipation was seen. It was a very important established fact which the women's movement could look to for support when tackling the next stage.

WORK ISN'T ALWAYS LIBERATING

While China is almost the only country in the world today where the vast majority of women participate in social production, this didn't come about smoothly. Some figures are worth thinking about. For example in Shanghai in 1966, on the eve of the Cultural Revolution, more than half the women had given up their jobs and had returned to their domestic lives. This can be explained partly by the policy of the Chinese Communist Party, under the influence of Liu Shao-chi, ex-presidents of the People's Republic of China, which involved waging an intensive propaganda campaign for a return to the home. This took many and varied forms. Here a mother's 'unique' ability to raise children was praised; there it was stated outright that women were good for nothing, too limited intellectually to learn a trade. The scarcity of day-care centres and canteens was often used as an argument against women working. As for those who already had a job, their work was interpreted in a particular way: a second wage for that little bit extra ('work to feed and clothe your family better')![1] This reactionary chorus was no doubt loud enough to discourage many whose intentions were good. But by itself it cannot explain the fairly widespread return to the home. We must look for the underlying reasons in the work itself, in its organization. Otherwise it's hard to understand how women holding down a job as part of their effort to liberate themselves could have allowed themselves to be convinced by such backward-looking theories. It's really because not all the working women were actually gaining any freedom. Wherever there were genuinely liberating jobs women didn't leave the factories in such great numbers. In the Chao Yan factory, which we visited, only about ten women 'went back behind their front doors', as the Chinese say.

Nobody can still think that the Soviet way of explaining things is satisfactory: 'Here is a state-owned factory, and since the State is the Party and the Party is the masses, the factory belongs to the workers, QED.' That's no longer acceptable. If I'm told, 'This factory belongs to you and the people' while I blindly obey bosses' orders, understanding nothing about my machine and even less about the rest of the factory; if I don't know what happens to my product when it's finished, or *why* it was produced in the first place; if I have to work faster to get a bonus; if I'm bored to death in the factory waiting all week for Sunday, all day for clocking-off time; if I'm even more ignorant after years of working than when I began – then it's because the factory is neither mine nor the people's! When production is still organized on capitalistic lines, that is maintaining and deepening the separation between intellectual and manual work and sticking to the rule of profitability; when production relies on a bourgeois rule-book, blind discipline and material incentives and maintains a division between those who think on one side and those who do on the other – then the least educated, especially the women, are also the most oppressed.

A significant number of women were convinced of the advantages of returning to domesticity, because in the first place the class struggle had not yet defeated the bourgeoisie in the factories. Because of this, work remained subject to bourgeois criteria. And capitalist production can no more 'liberate' women than it has ever actually liberated men. We, who had all worked in factories, remembered the endless conversations with other women on the subject: 'If my husband earned enough, I'd stay at home', 'When I get married, I won't work any more.' Such talk came up again and again, even though, the very next day, these same women would swear: 'I wouldn't stay at home for anything in the world, I'd get too bored.' Such wavering opinions only reveal the particularly ambiguous position of women workers in a capitalist country: they have enough experience of social labour to appreciate the triviality of housework, but this social labour itself is so devoid of meaning as to make the prospect of staying at home seem like a temporarily inaccessible luxury. A solderer in a television factory once told me: 'On Monday morning, the prospect of the whole week ahead of me makes me envy those who can stay at home; on Sunday evening, after a day of cleaning-up, I pity them.'

Yet while the participation of women in social labour has not liberated them, it has nevertheless been a decisive factor in arousing an awareness of their oppression and in the socialization of their rebellion. It has led to an enormous increase in their consciousness of oppression: 'woman's condition' or the misfortune of being a woman.

1 The Chinese Road to Industrialization and Women's Liberation

NO WORK, NO PAY. THEY STAYED IN THE FACTORY!

The Chao Yan Medical Apparatus Factory in Peking isn't much to look at – a few brick buildings opening out on to a yard reminiscent of a school playground. Yet things are happening there, with little fuss being made, which are critical for the future of women. We were received there two or three days after our arrival, seated round a long table, in a little white room, our cold fingers hugging scalding cups. A woman worker in her fifties, Ma Yu-yin, told us the history of the factory:

'Until 1958 most women in this neighbourhod used to stay at home and work for their family, doing housework, looking after children ... It was then that the whole country rose up to make the "great leap forward", and everyone's energies were mobilized for the next step in the transformation of society. In the countryside, the peasants were reorganizing the more advanced co-operatives into people's communes; industry was being widely decentralized; and even in the most remote areas small industries were springing up. Were we, the women, to stay at home, out of the storm? Chairman Mao appealed to us 'to rely on our own strength, to break away from our housework and participate in productive and social activities'. We wanted to answer this call, to make the great leap forward too. But how could we go about it? It was then that about twenty women in this neighbourhood decided to 'cross the threshold of the home' and set up a local factory. The street committee let us have two empty warehouses for this. From one point of view everything seemed to be working against us: there weren't many of us, we had no equipment, no crèche, no canteen, no experience of production (we were all housewives). We didn't even know what to make. But on the other hand we held important trump cards. We hadn't decided to work just to make life a bit more comfortable for our families: we wanted to change society, to transform the condition of women. If only women would throw open the doors of their houses, which block their view! We no longer wanted to serve our families, we wanted to serve the people.

'Finally, after asking round the district, we decided to make essential goods such as kettles, stove-pipes, saucepans, that sort of thing. We brought our own tools from home: hammers, pliers, a few screwdrivers, nails and so on. We had nothing else. We went to factories to salvage sheets of scrap metal and iron tubes, and we set to work. Sometimes some workers would come in after work to show us what to do. A serious problem of another kind was looking after the children.

'For example this comrade here had five children. We managed as best we could. The older children looked after the younger ones. Some women could leave their children in the care of their mothers or mothers-in-law. There were neighbours, too, who approved of what we were doing and gave us a hand. You could say that the problem was solved during that period by mutual aid. During the whole time we didn't get any wages. We would often stay at the factory even until late into the night to finish some task we had set ourselves.'

Broaden Production, Deepen Knowledge

'Finally, by a process of trial and error, we succeeded in making kettles and stove-pipes by hand. These products were accepted by the State. That was our first victory. A few ordinary, unskilled housewives helping one another had actually managed, by dint of sheer energy and obstinacy, to manufacture household appliances of a high enough quality for the State to buy. We redoubled our efforts. We next decided to diversify according to the needs of the people. We asked round to find out what the new local needs were, and then we began to manufacture medical apparatus: protective sheets for use with X-ray machines, isolating cabinets. We used old discarded machines; we took them apart, repaired them and converted them ourselves because it was more productive and easier that way. This work was more complicated and required more knowledge than kettle-making.

'We had posted up in the workshop Chairman Mao's saying: 'Times have changed, and today whatever men comrades can accomplish, women comrades can too.' There was no fundamental reason why women couldn't build this apparatus. Sometimes some of us would become discouraged in the face of the difficulties. They used to say: 'What's the use of all these efforts, we'll never succeed. We're not educated, medical apparatus is too difficult to make, we'd better stick to kettles'. We would discuss it among ourselves. 'We aren't here to make money for ourselves and even less are we here to enrich some boss. The people need this apparatus. Should we women hang our heads when faced with the risk of failure? For centuries and centuries Chinese women have been treated like animals. We are part of the working class. How can it lead the country if half of it is kept ignorant and unable to learn new techniques? We don't know anything! Okay then, let's learn! The most beautiful stories are written on blank pages!' And we would return to the task, our confidence restored. With the help of other factories who sent skilled people to advise us we managed to produce not only protective sheets and isolating cabinets, but also large high-temperature sterilizers and infra-red lamps. After an inspection, the

State gave us the job of producing those things and our factory took the name it has now: the Chao Yan Medical Apparatus Factory. By then our ranks had swelled and there were just over three hundred of us, including about twenty men. In 1960 we built four more workshops in the yard without asking the State for a single penny, simply by salvaging bricks from old buildings. That same year we built a restaurant and a crèche in the factory enclosure. All this with our own hands; we can built socialism with our hands.'

An Example Of Successful Feminine Resistance

'Inside the factory there was a feeling of solidarity, dynamism and dedication. It was quite common to see women workers staying on after their day's work to finish a job, or to practise a difficult technique. Of course we weren't forced to do that, and we weren't paid for the overtime. Must we get bonuses for making the revolution? And that was what it was about. Besides, our experiment didn't by any means please everybody. In 1961 some of the factory's managers, completely blinded by orders from the Peking town council,[1] decided to "rationalize" production. They decreed that there were too many of us working there and that we would have to stop making kettles since we were now a medical-apparatus factory. How contemptuous they were about our kettles! The 'reorganisation' would have meant a good number of us returning home. They thought they'd convince us by saying that the men would get a wage rise so that we could stay at home and look after our families. Wouldn't everything be simpler that way? But these plans encountered spirited resistance from the women, and they declared: "We won't go back to our cooking, we won't give up our jobs!" Life in the factory became very tense. There was a desperate struggle between that faction of the management who wanted the factory to be run for immediate profit and who, above all, didn't want the women workers to liberate themselves, and the large majority of women workers who wanted to continue on their chosen path.

'This struggle was fought in full awareness of what it was all about. We understood what was at stake. In most cases our husbands and the other men supported us. That can easily be explained. What happened in Chao Yan wasn't an isolated incident. In all the factories a reactionary offensive arranged by Liu Shao-chi aimed either to re-establish capitalist norms of production, or to prevent their overthrow by the masses. This explains why the men, who were also having to confront the bourgeois offensive, understood and generally backed up the women's resistance. Since many of us were out of work, we got no pay. But it didn't matter. If we didn't have any work, we would make some for ourselves! If we got no wages, we would hang on by helping one another! We asked other factories to give us work that we would then do in "our factory". Some women workers would bring scrap to the factory (bricks, sheet metal and so on) and we salvaged and cleaned it for recycling. The women's work was *useful*, even if it wasn't "profitable", and we proved it. A few women, only about fifteen of us, were unable to go through with it. They either went to work in large factories or returned home. During the Cultural Revolution we came to understand even more clearly the real nature of this reactionary policy. We led campaigns to denounce the method of so-called "rationalization". Most of those who had supported Liu Shao-chi's line discovered the interests they had really been serving. They are now working side by side with us. Almost all the women who had left the factory have come back to work here. Recently the women workers at this factory have perfected a process for the manufacture of silicon. Previously the workers here were all former housewives and generally quite old, between forty and fifty. Now we also have some young school-leavers, who share their knowledge with the older workers, at the same time learning from them the qualities of revolutionary persistence and proletarian resilience. In this neighbourhood virtually none of the women stays home, only the women who are too old or who are in bad health — but even for them life has changed. They help one another, and take on a few domestic chores to relieve the ones who have jobs away from home; they organize the political and cultural life of the district; they aren't as isolated as before. This transformation is the result of the move by thousands of women into productive and social activities. As for us, we are wage-earners, and it's important that we have won our economic independence. But it must be understood that it is still more important for us to stand four-square in the world, to be concerned about communal affairs rather than to care only about family problems. We have used production as a weapon to liberate ourselves, to serve the Chinese people and world revolution better.'

More About Small Street Factories

There are thousands of small district factories like Chao Yan in China. The first wave of factory building came at the time of the 'great leap forward'. These factories came under relentless fire from Liu Shao-chi and many were shut down. During the Cultural Revolution new ones mushroomed everywhere. They now form a dense, widespread network of industrial production, across the whole of China, by which China works, breathes and lives. As the small Chao Yan Factory proves beyond doubt, little or no investment is needed to start them because they depend entirely on living labour and on the workers' political determination and creativity. They also have the advantage of close ties with the local community, understanding its specific difficulties as well as the immediate needs of the people. The women of the Chao Yan district in Peking both wanted to work collectively at useful jobs and had the will to transform the living reality of the neighbourhood. If the housewives, in their determination to 'get out of the family', had simply gone to work in big factories outside the district, the main result would have been to turn their neighbourhood into a dormitory suburb. What actually happened, as Ma Yu-yin pointed out to us, was that when small factories were built in the heart of the district new relationships and new activities developed in the neighbourhood. The factories gave the neighbourhoods new life and their influence really spread throughout the whole district.

We saw these small factories in the countryside and in the cities. A factory stands with all its doors wide open just off the main road among the houses, helping to set the rhythm of the days and the nights for the people who live there, whether or not they work in it. Those who have retired help to run the small factories by organizing collective child-minding after school.

The struggle to build and develop these small factories has led women to face the problem of housework and often to open communal restaurants and crèches. Men become more committed to sharing household duties when the factories are at stake. Sanitation systems are built round the factories, benefiting the factory workers and the whole communities. Adults, and especially women, who go back to school most often go to learn about the problems they have encountered in factory production.

In destroying the artisan class, capitalism also destroyed the symbiotic relationship it had with consumers. Traditionally, craft production was necessarily closely bound up with local needs. While the Chinese neighbourhood factories have put an end to small-scale individual production, they have on the other hand retained and possibly strengthened their links with the consumers. This holds good not only for factories producing household appliances such as saucepans and chairs, but also for the manufacture of machinery and farm tools. This kind of industrial development is particularly conducive to the participation of women in social production. It doesn't demand any prior technical qualifications which the women happen not to have, but only their initiative and their knowledge of the actual needs of the people. Who are better suited to transform the daily life of a neighbourhood than those women who have assured it for so long? And who is better able to bring to the fore the use-value of an object instead of treating it simply as a commodity, those who worked for centuries to maintain, clean, prepare and make something that would be useful for their families rather than something that would pay? Despite the intolerable oppressiveness of this work from which their revolt stemmed, women have developed an acute sense of *useful work* which cannot be measured in profits, surplus value and labour time. When women come together to re-examine the meaning of work designed to serve privatized units, when society as a whole engages in a relentless struggle against private interest, then the time is ripe for those 'feminine qualities' so long repressed to shine out brilliantly.

Forging the dialectical links between the immediate needs of the people and the growth of a modern industry is no mean task. We are all aware how the Soviet Union waged great ideological campaigns: the sacrifice of a generation would guarantee a happy future. But for the mass of the Soviet people the music of the future turned out to be pure lamentation. The crushing priority accorded to heavy industry left without a solution the problem of what the masses were to consume. It was women who suffered most in the interminable queuing for scarce consumer goods and from the need to fall back on their own resources in order to maintain, somehow or other, a minimum standard of living. Had China followed that road to industrialization we can bet that Chinese women, and most of the men as well, would be no better off than unskilled workers in a reserve pool of labour. They wouldn't have become what they are today — informed workers who are changing the world in the process of changing themselves.

Technological developments should never be underestimated, even when they're not directed at the immediate creation of productive capacity. The great merit of Chinese industrialization has been that it has allowed all workers to be active in the growth of the productive forces. Chao Yan is a good example of the way in which the acquisition of the most advanced technology has been solidly founded on the progress of the workers. Former housewives with hardly any education progressed within eight years from making kettles to making sterilizers and, finally, to producing electronic equipment.

Ma Yu-yin told us: 'We have managed to master complex manufacturing processes with the help of large factories.' This is how it happens: to train its own technicians, the small neighbourhood factory sends a few women workers to the larger factories, where they work on recently developed machines with technicians and experienced workers. There they acquire useful new knowledge. When they return to the factory they set up "technological innovation teams" with other women workers, who work together to surmount the obstacles resulting from their lack of facilities and training.

Compared to the very recent past, productive forces in China are bounding ahead, and yet they can be, and are, more and more closely controlled by the people. How could the working class exercise power if it had only a narrow, fragmented knowledge of production and was 'under the domination of technology'? Through the revolution in social production, women in China have gained a thoroughgoing knowledge of society that was denied them as long as they stayed by their own firesides. Their participation in power is effective and not merely formal — and it is precisely on that that their liberation is based.

SUCHOW: ON 'FEMININE QUALITIES'

Although there are women in all sectors of the economy in China, many can still be found doing 'woman's work', in the health, education and textile sectors, for example. This is generally considered to be a temporary state of affairs, bound to be progressively phased out. I say 'generally' because this is by no means a unanimous opinion. We met several people who didn't seem to have considered the question very much, and were quite happy with the current situation. A male official in one factory told us with some pride that there were women doing all different kinds of jobs in the factory, and he concluded by quoting Mao Tse-tung's famous dictum: 'Whatever men comrades can accomplish, women comrades can too.' Chantal replied: 'That's all very well, but we've just come from the factory's crèche, and we didn't see any men looking after the children. Why not?' A fairly heated argument started among the Chinese comrades. He then replied; 'You see, it's because women have wonderful qualities when it comes to child-rearing'.

'Then you believe in the idea of innate and unchangeable human nature?' Chantal asked ironically.

'No, of course not!' he said abruptly, visibly offended. 'That's not what I meant.' He hesitated a moment, while laughter broke out all round him, then he replied: 'Comrade Chantal's remarks are quite correct, and I thank her for criticizing my inadequacies. The class struggle doesn't stop with socialism; if you come back to see us in a few years, you'll certainly find that great changes have taken place, and in particular there'll be men in the crèche.' He added: 'We shouldn't just say "Whatever a man comrade can accomplish a woman comrade can too", but also "What a woman comrade can accomplish, a man comrade can and must accomplish too."'

The 'feminine' virtues, not those supposedly given us by nature but those which stem from women's oppression, our heritage from the past, can in some cases be transformed and provide the impetus for a change in the condition of women. We were to witness a particularly clear example of this at the embroidery factory in Suchow.

Embroidering For The Revolution

A long time ago Suchow was renowned for its embroidery. But the embroideress used to work at home, and she was invariably very poor. After the liberation, in Suchow, as all over China, the Chinese Communist Party (CCP) recommended that women should participate in social production. A few factories could have been built in the town and women encouraged to work in them, but the local revolutionary leadership decided on a different policy. There were hundreds of embroideresses in Suchow who had become very good at their work. For generations they had been ruining their eyesight embroidering flowers and butterflies on the clothes of wealthy landlords. Should an art that the propertied class had appropriated be destroyed, or should it be transformed and restored to the people? The decision was probably not reached without a struggle. The idea of 'socializing' embroidery was certainly not an article of faith for the workers' movement in the 1950s. A mechanistic interpretation of Marx might imply that a production process could not be socialized unless it had previously been mechanized. But this 'heresy' didn't worry the communist women of Suchow. As plants need water, so the Chinese people needed an art for themselves. The embroideresses were useful to the people. Let no one tell them that this country – with some hundreds of millions of inhabitants and with an economy still underdeveloped, which had scarcely begun the task of overcoming the ancient and man-made curses of famine and war – needed machines more than art. Without art, there can be no revolution!

In Suchow, just as in Chao Yan, it was the determination of a small group of women (eight in all) that eventually brought about the co-operation of the majority. They had to resist a great deal of hostility from the home embroideresses.

In the first place, techniques had been handed down from generation to generation, and each embroideress jealously guarded some family secret. Co-operation meant sharing the tricks of the trade and therefore devaluing her individuality. In the same way, designs had in the past to be original to be of value; what would happen if anyone could reproduce a design? And then working at home has its advantages. You could, for example, embroider and mind the children at the same time. The eight 'feminists' weren't seduced by these arguments. They picked up their silk, scissors, needles and children and began to embroider together. They pooled everything, their experience, their initiative and their enthusiasm.

Far from becoming boring and unoriginal, their designs achieved a new variety through their work, and this change could be seen after only a few months. They would sketch together, discuss, criticize and improve their designs. The eight women embroidered more varied and more beautiful designs than a hundred embroideresses each locked up in her own home. They made similarly spectacular technical progress. Until then people had embroidered only one side of the silk; these women perfected a way of embroidering both sides, giving a lot of depth to the design and increasing the possibilities for relief work. Within a year the co-operative had grown from eight to a hundred members.

At that time there were still some capitalists in China (small capitalist enterprises continued to exist under strict state control until 1956) and the silk merchants in Suchow didn't look kindly on this battalion of angry women. They tried to smash the movement by increasing the price they offered for the embroideries. For example, the silk merchants would pay 24 fens for an embroidered pillow that the State bought from the co-operative for 20 fens, but on condition that the pillows should be made at home. This method was not as successful as expected. In fact it opened the eyes of many women. 'Had anyone ever seen a capitalist increase workers' wages without their asking for it? Clearly something peculiar was afoot.' The co-operative's ranks closed. While single, isolated embroideresses had always been at the mercy of the demands of the silk merchants and of their own mutual competition, the co-operative was soon able to guarantee its members a regular income from the sale of embroidery, with some state aid. They earned the right of all Chinese workers to free medical care and they organized a crèche and kindergarten in the gardens surrounding the workshops. Funds they had built up enabled them to expand production. They bought large silk stretchers (wooden frames, hinged on their supports, on which the silk is stretched for embroidering) and were able to embroider large designs on which several women could work together.

The fact that women aspired to become involved with art was politically significant. After all, it had been a long-established fact that women didn't understand the first thing about art, since art is creation and in matters of creation the weaker sex cannot raise itself above the level of procreation! What a cheek to assert that workers, and what's more women workers, could begin to understand these matters! Who were to be served, the people or their enemies? Should ancient tradition be upheld or should they introduce innovations? Should they depict kings and emperors or workers on the march? The controversy raged. On the pretext of preserving rich traditions, some women, still in the grip of bourgeois ideology, said that you couldn't portray the rough hands of peasants with fine thread. Their view was that trying to improve technique was more important than revolutionizing content. That's why until the Cultural Revolution most embroidery still depicted the heroes of the past, so dear to the Parisian antique dealers.

But it soon became clear that the position these women were defending was wrong even in relation to matters of technique. For example they would allow most of the embroideresses to work only on backgrounds, leaving the faces for the select few who knew how to embroider them and who would do it secretly, to maintain their prerogative. The other embroideresses, who had no hope of doing anything but backgrounds and headless bodies, were disgusted. The women had lost control of the factory and managerial decisions were actually being made by a team of 'experts' without any regard for the women's wishes and aspirations. A young embroideress tells the story:

'Since childhood I had had a burning desire to embroider on silk the faces of the revolutionary heroes who liberated China. But people made fun of me: "You're too young, you don't even know how to embroider the sky and the landscape properly, let alone eyes and noses! You're too ambitious!" I tried anyhow, on my own, and failed. Full of bitterness, I went back to doing skies and landscapes. During the Cultural Revolution we decided that doing faces would no longer be a special prerogative, a privilege. We would all be able to do them. So all the embroideresses had to be taught how. We made a lot of attempts, not always very successfully. Once I had embroidered a sentry squatting in the dark and watching out for the enemy. I wanted to convey the atmosphere of heavy silence and stillness that you feel when you hear descriptions of these scenes. But my friends burst out laughing when they saw my embroidery: "Your sentry must have been running hard. He's all out of breath, he's purple in the face, he must be puffing and blowing like an ox. The enemy must be deaf if they can't hear him!" That made me sad, but then my friends told me seriously, "It doesn't matter; if we don't try, we'll never win. Let's start again together, and this time make sure we don't use too much red. We'll get there in the end." In fact, although it's pretty difficult, we can all do faces well now, because we try to help one another and we no longer hide our work from one another.'

There are now 1600 embroideresses in this factory. We saw young men sitting at their frames embroidering with women advising them. Edith asked one of them: Don't you mind doing woman's work?'

'Not at all, I like it. And it isn't woman's work. That's the old society's way of seeing it: man's work, woman's work. Times have changed.'

'But don't the other men make fun of you?'

'No, embroidery is useful for the revolution. Of course there are still some people who think it's woman's work', and he added, smiling, 'The class struggle isn't over yet, we must keep fighting.'

THE STRUGGLE AGAINST THE SEPARATION OF MANUAL WORK FROM INTELLECTUAL WORK, AND WOMEN'S LIBERATION

It was while visiting a large textile factory in Changsha, where more than seven thousand workers (80 per cent of them women) are employed, that we suddenly understood what had until then seemed very confusing: just how changing the relationship between intellectuals and workers in the heart of the factories can contribute so enormously to women's liberation.

Our visit to the factory had to be short that day because we had a heavy schedule. We raced through the workshops filled with the noisy rattle of the shuttles. Afterwards, in the meeting-room, we weren't paying much attention. Then we heard: 'Before the Cultural Revolution there were more than 2500 rules and regulations aimed at oppressing the women workers in our factory.' Danielle asked the serious-looking young woman worker who had just spoken: 'Can you tell us how these rules acted against the women workers?' She answered without a moment's hesitation: 'Because of these absurd rules, women workers just couldn't make any technical innovations. If they wanted to improve production, their project had to pass through a complicated and intimidating hierarchy. When it finally reached a technician's desk, he usually wouldn't see any point in it and would throw it in the waste-paper basket. The system was discouraging and slowed down the development of production.'

I can still see the looks of disappointment and surprise we exchanged when we heard this. The first illustration of the repression of women workers that came to her – the fact that they weren't given enough opportunity to develop production – seemed to us to be stereotyped and unconvincing, to say the least.

Danielle changed the subject: 'Are women workers allowed to move to different jobs often enough to learn what the work is like everywhere?' 'We try to make it easy for women to work at different jobs with different people,' was the reply. 'But it's fairly difficult. Some jobs demand a lot of experience, so the older women can change round more easily than the younger ones. Even though we always try to make these changes possible, we don't consider them crucial. To get an overall knowledge of what goes on, it is essential to participate more and more in the work of development and design. In each workshop there is a technical innovation team made up of women workers, technicians and revolutionary cadres. As well as doing their shop-floor work, the team members plan projects and produce blueprints, scale models and drawings. The team takes up workers' daily suggestions, criticisms and advice. In this way knowledge and manual work, theory and practice, intellectuals and workers are gradually united. And the two sides of the old gap — which still exists, of course, but which is decreasing — are qualitatively transformed. The goal is to make a new man who will be unlike either the intellectuals or the workers of the past, who will neither be cut off from practice, the work and its concrete problems, nor lack theoretical understanding.

'Change is needed on both sides, but that is possible only if the workers themselves assume political and ideological leadership. They instruct one another, but it's really the workers who re-educate the intellectuals. It seems paradoxical, doesn't it? A long time ago we thought it was the duty of intellectuals to give 'knowledge' to the workers. That's a one-sided point of view. While it's true that a worker's knowledge is fragmented, at least it's knowledge tested by practice and based on a revolutionary class position.'

That's why the workers must lead in bringing about this change. If they are to free themselves from the limitations of their own knowledge, they must also liberate the intellectuals. Once again a specific case has illustrated Marx's thesis: 'Only by emancipating all mankind can the proletariat achieve its own final emancipation.' Each different job is like a cog in a big machine, and by jumping from one to the other, workers can widen the range of their practical experience. But they can never cross the boundary between the conception of an overall project and its practical realization. This explanation by the woman at Changsha really clarified what she had told us earlier: women workers really had suffered because they couldn't make technical innovations and give their initiative free reign.

We understand all that, you might say, but what does it have to do with women specifically?

Actually it's very simple, and you will understand, as we did. When we distinguish between manual and intellectual labour, the vast majority of women are traditionally manual workers. Not only because, like male workers, they haven't got enough information, but also because they are shut in by the family and thus even further removed than anyone else from any overall view of the world. Their world is their kitchen, the children's room and the conjugal bed. They are the semi-skilled workers of the home.

When they leave their homes to work in conventional factories, they are therefore, even more than their male colleagues, reduced to the role of carrying out 'mysterious orders'. But for the same reasons, they are the first to benefit from the revolutionary change in the relations between intellectuals and workers.

When the oppression of women stems, as it does, from their being cut off from social activities and therefore deprived of a social vision, there can be no solution but to give them immediate access to the widest and most comprehensive range of scientific information. This should not be handed down from teacher to pupil, but instead free reign should be given to the co-operative effort of intellectuals and women workers.

The acquisition of new skills and the diversification of practical experience are other important ways in which workers can develop that broad knowledge of things that was previously forbidden them. It's well known that some Chinese workers become doctors by being given practical and theoretical training by qualified doctors in the field, and not by going to university, but there are many other similar cases. For example workers will often go into the country for a few months to help set up small local industries, or to train peasants to become the skilled workers a commune needs. There are also groups of workers selected by fellow-workers to go — usually for a year to direct political and ideological work in all sorts of places besides factories: theatres, hospitals, schools, administrative offices, department stores.

They can also take up or continue studying and may, for instance, be chosen by other workers in their factory to go to university, to evening classes or to one of the part-time study centres set up in some factories, such as the one in a Shanghai machine-tool factory, where workers spend half the day on the shop floor and the other half studying.

The aim of technical-innovation teams, as with job diversification, is to close the gap between manual and intellectual work. Because the oppression of women is closely linked to this gap, their participation in the revolutionary social movement aimed at its abolition opens the way to their own liberation.

'EQUAL WORK, EQUAL PAY': SIMPLE IN PRINCIPLE BUT COMPLICATED IN PRACTICE

Comrade Pai, secretary of the revolutionary committee of the Sino-Albanian Friendship People's Commune, explained to us how ideas of 'absolute egalitarianism' ended up oppressing women yet again. Some men opposed the idea of women getting equal wages in the name of equality and the equal pay principle, saying: 'They don't do equal work, they don't carry loads as heavy as ours.' Pai told us that such ideas, held by only a minority but not uncommon, expressed the new society's struggle between the capitalist and the socialist roads. 'They must be criticized and vigorously opposed, because they are the tenets of a feudal approach towards women and work. In spite of countless real and historically important facts, the minority still, wrongly believe that women are inferior beings whose contribution to society is minimal. As for work, only slave-traders and exploiters judge human and animal labour by the same standards and with the same values – in terms of sheer physical force. Tibetan landowners, for instance, found that they could trade one healthy and physically strong slave for two less sturdy ones. In the new society, following the example of

Tachai,[2] we must first of all look at a person's political attitudes to society and to his or her work, regardless of sex, before we can determine the contribution his or her work makes.'

The controversy concerning the value of the work that women do has been the subject of an ongoing debate all over the country, as is shown by a *Red Flag*[3] article of February 1972:

> People have differing capacities for physical work. Farm labour which demands great physical strength should be left to men who have this strength. It is natural to take account of the physiologival' differences between men and women in allocating jobs. [As for differences among women themselves, we were often told that work demanding great physical strength is not given to weak men or women in poor health. Author's note]. ... But in no case whatsoever must the degree of physical strength be used to justify wage differentials between men and women. Following the principle *to each according to his or her abilities and to his or her work* the norms which determine wages take into account the actual quantity and quality of each worker's labour, as well as his or her greater or lesser contribution to socialist production.[4]

A concern with the specific physiological characteristics of women is also revealed in rest-day and holiday arrangements. Everyone has at least one day off a week, but women, whether in the town or country, get four extra days a month when they have their period. Women also retire at fifty or fifty-five, depending on the type of work they've been doing, while men retire at about sixty. The distinction between absolute egalitarianism and equality between the sexes may seem a little too fine or dangerously fuzzy round the edges, threatening to introduce a notion of equality based on 'nature', propped up by physiology. Indeed how do we know which sex differences are purely physiological and which are acquired, and at least partly determined by the role women play in society? The dividing line isn't easy to draw, but it has to be drawn somewhere.

The same controversy about 'male and female work' crops up in connection with the question of whether women have the ability to master certain agricultural jobs. Some people (apparently opposing the 'egalitarians') go so far as to assert that men and women must share the work according to their sex. The same article in *Red Flag* comments:

> The division of agricultural labour into male and female jobs is a left--over of the old society which still survives in some regions. For example jobs requiring more complex technological skills like the sowing of wheat and rice or soil fertilization have in the past been considered man's work. Some people still refuse to allow women to learn these jobs or to participate in them. Some simply mock the women who do take up these jobs, saying that it's 'topsy-turvy' or 'the world is back-to-front'.

The article points out that men have become better equipped to do this work only because they've been practising it for so long, while women in the old society were confined to domestic tasks, and were generally not allowed to do work in the fields and on the farm.

Red Flag comments further: 'Why couldn't women, with practice, also master the technique of transplanting seedlings? Where does technique come from if not from practical experience? Such attitudes are part of a feudal mentality. They are a manifestation of the contempt in which the exploiting classes hold women. It is this notion of women's nature, a pernicious and reactionary notion, to which Liu Shao-chi and others referred.' The effects these attitudes would have on wages for both men and women are then discussed:

> There is another kind of mistaken idea which must be fought. Some comrades admit that in fact it is wrong for women to get eight points [5] for doing the same work as brings ten points for men. And yet they do nothing to eliminate this wrong, reasoning that, 'If you look at wages from the point of view of a household rather than from an individual point of view, you see that nobody actually suffers financially because each family is made up of men and women.' This sort of thinking leads its exponents to give the wrong emphasis to the application of the equal pay principle . . . It is incorrect reasoning because the problem cannot be seen from the standpoint of household profit or loss. The implementation of the principle of equal pay for equal work is first of all a very important political problem and a problem of ideology. Economic equality of the sexes is closely linked to political equality. The fact that the old ideology of male superiority and female inferiority still survives in some pockets of the country is nothing but the political image of the economic inequality between men and women. In fact the struggle of the mass of women against inequality is carried out on the political level. Some women put it very well when they say, 'We are not struggling for a few extra work points, we are struggling for dignity.' To consider that unequal pay for men and women is not a fundamental problem is tantamount to considering that the status of women is of only secondary importance – an attitude which is part of the feudal ideology of contempt for women!

2 The Socialization of the Chinese Countryside and Women's Liberation

PEASANT WOMEN TELL THEIR STORY

In the meeting-room of the Shawan peoples' commune a peasant woman in her forties told us how the commune's land had become collectivized, a process which was marked at each stage by the role played by women.

'At the time of the liberation the agrarian reform politically emancipated the poor and middle peasants – and women, like men, were given land. But the family was still the unit of production, and had to manage on its own when there were difficulties. One year there was a big drought, and if we were going to harvest anything at all we had to carry our water to the fields. Those families who were short-handed were at a great disadvantage. A widow I know had received five mous [1 mou is 1/15 hectare] during the agrarian reform but as she had no help her income was very low. She thought about the nature and root of her difficulties and took an active part in setting up the first mutual-aid groups between families. But these groups didn't resolve everything. We helped one another, but as long as production was based on family property, it was the family who bore the final responsibility for their own successes or failures. One year a neighbouring family was seriously hit by illness; they couldn't work and eventually had to sell their land [the right to sell land lasted until 1952] to buy medicine. This was an important political lesson for all the poor peasants in the village. We thought: 'Class distinctions will just get more pronounced unless we work harder at collectivization.' So we set up the first co-operatives. Several families worked together and divided the profits according to the amount of land and livestock contributed. Women were doubly attracted to this co-operation. Firstly, as peasants they knew that it was the only way to keep the countryside from becoming a hell for the exploited poor once again. And secondly they knew that as long as production centred on the family unit, they would be stuck at home. Who else could take care of the children, do the housework and cook the meals? But with teams, everyone, men and women alike, worked on the land, and problems with children and housework *had* to be solved on a collective basis.

' "If we help one another on the land, we must also help one another in the home – this was the position of the women. I myself told my husband: "We must join this co-operative." But he only replied: "You're nothing but a mare [a term for a woman dating from the old society]. You don't understand anything about these things and you won't got out to work!" I used to get really angry: "Women have liberated themselves, you have absolutely no right to treat me like this. Everything we have, we have won through struggle and I won't give it up!" And I joined the co-operative without him. He had been a poor peasant, he owned a small plot, sometimes he couldn't do all the work on it himself and he would grumble about his difficulties. I would explain to him, giving him the facts, the advantages of the co-operative. Gradually, he realized that his stubborness stemmed from the feudal ideas he still had about private property and the role of women, and when he accepted that, he felt able to join the co-operative. I know many families in the village where things happened just like that.

'Later on we took another step towards collectivization More forces had to be brought together so that we could take on the large-scale projects that were necessary if we were to control the forces of nature, like building irrigation works for example. But instead of pushing for more collectivization, the Liuists [Liu Shao-chi's partisans] took advantage of every natural disaster to promote the nonsense of "the family as unit of production". They would launch into defeatist speeches or would say insolently that our commune was too small, with a workforce of two thousand, to carry out big projects like these. To arrive at a figure of two thousand, they counted two women as one man.

'The hills surrounding our brigade[1] were so arid and dry that they looked bald. The poorer peasants who wanted more collectivization would say: "Man must control nature and not the other way round. The bald hills will wear luxurious manes before long." And we began the struggle. Day after day we carried full baskets of earth to the hills on our backs. We dug terraces in the soil. One by one the four hills surrounding the commune came into our hands. Now we gather the largest tea harvest in the region from these hills. Could we ever have achieved results like that on separate little allotments? Our victories arm us with facts to fight the Liuists. And in this struggle the women are in the vanguard – and that's common knowledge.'

The secretary of the revolutionary committee, who was sitting next to her, spoke up. 'I should like to give you some other examples of how women often taught us revolutionary lessons in clear-sightedness and tenacity. Some time ago, before the irrigation works were built, there was a terrible drought. The entire harvest was at risk. We couldn't even contemplate transporting water because all the surrounding rivers had dried up. A few of the old people in the commune said they remembered that when they were kids there had been a spring in a large field near the village, but no one could remember exactly where it was. A team of girls decided to look for it. They set out at once for the field above the village. For five days and five nights they dug the earth to find it again. A lot of people thought their effort was useless, and made fun of it. Springs in Shawan! Never! But on the morning of the sixth day, the girls rushed into the village, shouting, "We've found the spring, we've found the spring!" Everyone ran to the spot and saw a little stream trickling over the ground. They had found it by feeling the earth with their hands until they came across lumps of earth that were slightly less dry. They went on digging on that spot, until they got to the spring. It wasn't easy. The whole village now started working; we spent all day digging a large reservoir, then we dug some canals. Within a week we had got enough water to irrigate the fields. Our crops ater with their bare hands because they were determined to prove that collectivism was better than private family ownership, whien are saying, another man will always remind them, "What about the spring? Who was right, the women or us? We must never forget the lesson of the spring!"'

After this meeting we were led up a narrow path to the spring. On the site they had dug a deep reservoir to hold 6000 litres and had lined the walls with stones. Edith imagined the six girls on all fours, going over every single centimetre of the field as if they were feeling someone's vast belly, so confident that they would succeed that they weren't even aware of the herculean dimensions of the task. Why didn't the men do this work? After all, women haven't got any special talent for water divination! And why were the poorest peasants the first to co-operate? Obviously their own economic situation meant that they were in the best position to appreciate the advantages of collectivism. The women spent five days looking for water with their bare hands because they were determined to prove that collectivism was better than private family ownership, which they *also* experienced as a concrete form of women's oppression.

There is too great a tendency to think that the specific nature of women is important only in relation to the contradictions between men and women. Actually the long experience of oppression with which women are familiar is more extensive than that. Let's assume that feminine specificity takes two forms, or more exactly that it has a dual nature. On the one hand women are seen as social inferiors (in a society based on private property). On the other hand, women are traditionally inferior in their day-to-day relationships with men – and this subjugation is a product of their social inferiority. Then, because women's view of the family is informed by this dual oppression, they have a much clearer idea of the limitations of the family unit, and they are more likely than men to reject the illusion that 'the ideal is to be master in one's own home'. Women have been the vanguard at certain moments in history because some of them, more than any other groups of people, have nothing to lose but their chains. The challenge of the Shawan dowsers can and *must* be understood only in this way. For women, who have always been most dominated by nature, to be in the front line in the struggle to control nature, what a marvellous reversal of history, what a defeat for the sceptics!

THE NEW WOMEN'S COMMITTEES IN SHAWAN

In the course of the same conversation the people of Shawan confirmed that during the Cultural Revolution the old women's organization had been 'suspended'. This old revolutionary group, born in the flames of the war against Japan, had become a sort of welfare organization pushing the reactionary women-in-the-home ideology, interested only in the tiny world of domestic bliss and sorrow, in the idea of the little woman we're so familiar with in the pages of capitalist women's magazines. Comrade Ton An-ming, a peasant in her thirties, told us that several revolutionary committees had been organized in Shawan, that about 5500 of the women from the people's commune – more than 80 per cent – belonged, and that she herself was one of the women in charge. During our visit we were often told that women's organizations had reached the stage of 'struggle/criticism/reform'. These groups were still taking stock of past activities and, moreover, new directions had not been clearly mapped out yet. Clearly the people as a whole were still debating the topic – a nationwide organization would not be created by a decision from above, but on the basis of a host of observations and investigations by the masses themselves. We were particularly interested, therefore, in finding out what aims (even if, as seemed probable, they were short-term ones) the Shawan women's revolutionary committees had decided on. Ton An-ming answered our query: 'At the moment we have agreed on five main tasks. First, *study of Marxism, of Leninism and of Mao Tse-tung's thought*. I'd like to tell you how we've gone about this. To start with we had mixed study groups. So couples would bring their small children with them, and this interfered with our studying. The women then suggested that instead of helping one another to baby-sit on a neighbourly basis, it would be better if the men stayed at home to look after the kids while the women studied. That way we are free to study, and besides the men have a clearer idea of what looking after children is all about. It's arranged so that the women and the men study separately, each for six sessions every month. The women are very well satisfied with this system. "We've found this to be an efficient way of studying politics", they say . . .'

Just then an old peasant women interrupted Ton An-ming to say: 'One evening I had to go out to study and it started to pour with rain. It was pitch-black. My husband said I shouldn't go out in such weather and in total darkness. I answered him that in the old days, in spite of the daylight, I had been as good as blind because, like almost all women, I couldn't read or write. Now that I was more than sixty and going to school again to share revolutionary experiences with other women, to re-educate myself and to raise the level of my political consciousness, did he want me to stay at home? I told him, "You don't know what we women would pay in order to study." I tell you this story because it shows that women really are set on studying politics," the old peasant woman ended, without having paused for breath. Although she was visibly embarrassed by speaking in public and in front of foreigners, she had decided to do it to make sure we would realize how vitally important this point was to her: *women have a burning desire to study.*

Ton An-ming carried on talking about the second task, which she said was to do *everything to facilitate the most far-reaching revolutionary critique.* 'We women must wage an all-embracing struggle against every manifestation of revisionism. In particular, we must follow through to its conclusion the mass criticism of the old aims of the women's organisation.' 'The third task,' she continued, 'is to *do everything to enable women to participate fully in all the various political activities, so that they fulfil their role as "half of heaven".* There are women in every area and at all levels of leadership, but there are still too many who daren't voice their opinions at a public meeting, and there are too many men who won't listen when such opinions are voiced. Our job is to investigate this problem, to mobilize the masses and to find a solution to it.'

I was reminded of some words spoken by the political instructor of a May 7 school [2] near Peking: 'Whenever a man and a woman are equally qualified to fill a responsible post, the policy of the party is to choose a woman comrade. This is a matter of revolutionary principle.'

'The fourth task is *to overcome reactionary ideas in women and men alike, particularly those connected with the alleged superiority of men in certain technical areas.* We see to it that women participate in all social activities without exception. We are ruthlessly struggling against superstitions which have been especially directed against women.'

This isn't just an empty phrase for comrade Ton, but a matter of hard reality. The miners of Shawan had told us that in the past women were supposed to bring bad luck, and if a woman was seen walking near a pit the workers would refuse to go down, believing that there was a curse on the pit. Another ancient precept forbade women to take wine offerings in religious temples. A woman who drank holy wine would die instantly, a victim of divine wrath. Rebellious women, struggling against obscurantism, drank some of this wine, watched by the frightened villagers, whose superstitious beliefs were deeply shaken when they were not promptly struck down.

Ton An-ming told us another story: 'A few years ago there was torrential rain; huge areas of crops were destroyed and cloudbursts washed away any sloping fields. A 500-kilogram rock was moved more than a kilometer in the storm. Hen, a class enemy, tried to dissuade the masses from acting. He went round saying, "When you see the torrent on the mountain slope, it always means that the god of the plague is descending on the earth. We must let him alone, otherwise everything will be laid waste." These feudal words confused some of the peasants. What's more, a few older ones almost believed that this was a punishment from heaven for the social changes they had made. So comrade Pin came forward and harangued the villagers: "The torrent is merely water. It's just the result of the heavy rain. What can it devastate? Houses and fields perhaps, but not, as Hen would have you believe, everything. It can't destroy our will to carry the revolution through to its conclusion. No force in the world can do that. Not only must we overcome this fear of punishment, we must also struggle with all our might to conquer natural disasters. If we redirect the torrent we can avoid further destruction of crops and houses. Let's set to work!." She organized the women to take on a good share of this work. After several days of strenuous activity we had moved more than 30,000 cubic meters of earth and had managed to control the torrent completely! And that year, in spite of the floods caused by the rains, we harvested 25,000 kilograms more than the previous year. The Shawan commune's poor and middle peasants have struggled against heaven, earth and class enemies, and have won through. Women have played a crucial part in every struggle, bearing out Mao Tse-tung's point that women are a decisive force for the victory of the revolution.

'Our fifth task is to *redouble our efforts to revolutionize ideas about the family*. Women have an important contribution to make to society in this area too. We've already had quite a lot of experience of it here. Maybe comrade Li Ma-shien can tell you about her own case.'

Li Ma-shien, about forty years old, with a suntanned face, began to speak: 'Once the brigade needed a table for the collective. When I found out about it I told the comrades I'd got a suitable one at home, and that they could take it. When my husband realized I had lent the table, he got angry and said, "Some women go to work to bring more things home for the family, but my wife does the opposite and gives our things away." After he'd said all this, I organized a meeting to study Mao Tse-tung's thought in our family. I particularly criticized Liu Shao-chi's revisionist line, according to which there is no contradiction between collective and private interest. This is a hypocritical idea and one that encourages selfishness. We poor peasants must serve the people totally. In spite of our personal interest, we must struggle against selfishness and try to develop for ourselves a proletarian conception of the world. We must learn to act first and foremost in the interests of the people. During the meeting my mother-in-law talked about past suffering and present happiness. She said: "What "Must we take pleasure selfishly, and think only about our own family, forgetting the past, and forgetting the seven hundred million Chinese and the three thousand million human beings who people the earth? Must we look to our own welfare and forget that two-thirds of humanity still live under the yoke of oppression and exploitation?" The whole thing moved my husband deeply. Now he puts collective property first and foremost and thinks of his own possessions only afterwards. When the comrades brought back the table some time later, my husband applied a little self-criticism and said, "Whenever the brigade needs anything, our house is always open." '

The revolutionary transformation of the family is an enormous task. It involves changing the social function of the family *and* destroying private interest, as well as progressively creating new relations between men and women, and radically changing relations between parents and children. That's why it's interesting to note that Chinese revolutionaries do not consider the evolution of the family to be a simple *consequence* of social upheaval, but a necessary precondition of the revolution. They feel that women are naturally responsible for 'leading' the revolution in the family and that this is one of the fundamental tasks that women must undertake for humanity. Ton An-ming concluded; 'We can summarize the revolutionary committee's goals as follows: under the leadership of the party and of Chairman Mao, we *must do everything possible to enable women to carry out fully their historical role.*' Make no mistake! The Chinese don't need to win women over to the revolution, still less to neutralize them. They simply need to let women play out their historical role, for without them the revolution will be abortive.

What will the new Chinese women's movement be like? Judging by the example of Shawan's committees and Mao Tse-tung's attitudes towards the subject, it will be rooted in the recognition of the remarkable contribution that women have made to the revolution. We are as far away from Liu Shao-chi's paternalism as we are from that dominant tendency in the Third International to see women as a backward and manipulable mass, who have to be pushed into action.

Part Two
SOCIALIZING HOUSEWORK

Introduction

One problem must be solved if we are to achieve equality between the sexes: housework must be transformed. I have been concerned, first of all, to trace how the fact that women began to participate in production played a decisive role in their emancipation, because I believe that this was the route actually taken by Chinese women towards their liberation. Women who have been confined to household tasks which keep them outside the mainstream of society will liberate themselves only by plunging straight into social production, as Ma Yu-yin said. But as long as it is the women who do the housework, this participation is in reality impossible. It's the same old vicious circle we know so well in Europe. Almost a century ago, Engels analysed it in very clear terms:

> Only modern large-scale industry again threw open to her – and only to the proletarian woman at that – the avenue to social production; but in such a way that, when she fulfils her duties in the private service of her family, she remains excluded from public production and cannot earn anything; and when she wishes to take part in public industry and earn her living independently, she is not in a position to fulfil her family duties ... The first premise for the emancipation of women is the reintroduction of the entire female sex into public industry; and ... this again in demands that the quality possessed by the individual family of being the economic unit of society be abolished. [1]

One aspect of the contradiction which affects the vast majority if women is necessarily of prime importance – the root of the whole contradiction, if you like – and this is the aspect of women's social role that must be attacked first.

The women workers of Chao Yan and Suchow didn't wait for the problem of child care to be solved for example, before becoming involved in social production. Yet if this problem hadn't been adequately solved in time, these women would have found themselves in the only too familiar position of European women – doing two jobs every day.

Comrade Su Yin, who accompanied us throughout our trip, was in her fifties and had been a member of the Chinese Communist Party for about thirty years. She had been one of the original members responsible for organizing women. She told us that she was with us to help us study and understand the role of women in the Chinese revolution. 'The socialization of housework is a key to women's liberation she told us. 'Unless we achieve this socialization, equality between the sexes will remain formal – existing in law but not in reality – the antagonism between men and women will not be resolved and, in the last analysis, socialism will fail. So it really is going to become a major issue for us.'

HOW THE WASHING MACHINE HAS FAILED TO EMANCIPATE WOMEN

I've always found it very instructive to listen to the official statements handed out by a truly naive bourgeois Establishment announcing that nowadays, the urban housewife spends the same average number of hours doing housework as the housewife of a hundred years ago. It's easy to believe it when you realize that a working-class woman with three children and 'not working' (as they say with magnificent hypocrisy) still spends about fourteen hours a day on housework. Regrettably, a hundred years ago the days contained only twenty-four hours, as they still do in our time, and our great-grandmothers would have been hard put to spend more than fourteen hours on *their* housework and come out alive at the end of each week. And yet industrialization of the vast majority of production on a massive scale has had an undeniable and truly remarkable impact on housework.

Let's take the obvious example of the almost exclusively family produced goods of four or five generations ago: clothes, preserved food, bread, and even woven material in some places. All these have simply vanished as the products of a housewife's domestic duties. And what you don't make, you buy these days, by courtesy of industrial capitalism. More recently, with mass production of household appliances, like automatic washing machines, we have been freed from many of the other routine aspects of housework. But if capitalism has really abolished all this drudgery, what do housewives find to do all day long? How many times have you heard some man ask that question? The truth is that we don't do *less*, we just do *different things* differently and, when all's said and done, in worse conditions. It may be true that *we* don't have to go to the wash-house any more to scrub and beat our washing by hand. But on the other hand our great-grandmothers weren't confronted by the impossible task of organizing their day round a husband's shift work, the children's schoolday and the opening hours of shops and post offices. They didn't have to spend several hours each day travelling to and from supermarkets which, although admittedly less expensive, also happen to be miles away. They didn't spend whole afternoons being tossed, like a ping-pong ball, from one office to the next, from one specialist to the next, from one desk to the next, to fill in forms enabling their eldest child to go to summer camp, to enrol their youngest child at a school to get an inadequate rent rebate, to renew an identity card or to sort out national insurance, to find a place to live, to be refused accommodation, to visit another address and be told, 'Sorry, too late, it's already taken', to take a young child to the welfare clinic, to queue all day just to be told, 'Come back tomorrow.' Our great-grandmothers may not have had crèches, but then the ones *we* have are so few and so

INTRODUCTION 37

pathetic they aren't worthy of the name. In the old days our great-grandmothers had their grandmothers nearby, if not in the same house. They had old friends in the neighbourhood to help out – theirs was a completely different life-style. The sociologists describe our lives in terms of 'the increasing mobility of the work force' and we really do live in a state of perpetual motion – changing cities and friends like we change shoes. We stay in one particular neighbourhood barely long enough to know it, let alone the people in it. Our parents live far away, too far to look after our children.

Years ago there may have been no running water, but when women went to the village wash-house at least they met other women and had a chance to discuss all manner of things important to them and to the village as a whole. Running water may have disposed of the chore, but at the same time a *social link* between women has been severed. Ever since, the labour of washday, done behind closed walls, has become 'invisible' and, socially speaking, non-existent.

Vacuum cleaners, refrigerators and washing machines – so what! You have to get into debt to buy them, and you'd need to be a technician to maintain and service them. So we take them to the 'expert'. 'Unfortunately,' the expert tells us, 'they don't make this model any more and there aren't any spare parts available.' The machine can't be mended, anyway. It's useless. Paul is good with machines, but he hasn't got time to fix it. But it seems we're in luck. The salesman graciously agrees to take it back. A worthless machine is suddenly revalued. We will get 50 francs for this scrap-metal vacuum cleaner, on the sole condition that we buy a new one for 250 francs. Mechanization on these lines is a two-edged weapon: on the one hand some jobs are made easier; but on the other hand it creates new ones. To be truly efficient, all kinds of labour-saving devices should be used collectively; no single family, and therefore no single woman, should bear the full responsibility for the new jobs of maintenance, repair and so on.

One successful and respectable Frenchwoman[2] made a startling discovery some years ago. Housework, she revealed, is like factory work. To do it properly you must have effective organization, sound financial support, job rationalization – in other words, everything required in the management of a small business. With skill and care, you might even show a profit! And the women who run this 'small business' are no longer servants to their household, but chairwomen! They will, of course, have worries, the author admits. After all, it's a well-known fact that no chair-*man* is without worries. But think of the enormous satisfaction of getting all the work done in six hours while the poor narrow-minded creatures who haven't yet grasped the historical scope of their role still toil for six and a half hours, or even seven. And what does she do, the housewife-manager of our friend's imagination, with all the time she's saved? She goes to the hairdresser to have her hair set so that she can please a husband who most probably won't even notice. What a thrill!

In the quite distant past women spent long, boring days doing their family's washing. They would set aside a day for the window-cleaning, and one for scrubbing the floors. They'd have a day for jam-making and another for ironing. These days a woman is more likely to spend her time making beds, shopping, preparing a meal, washing up, ironing, doing the washing, shopping again, cooking another meal, washing up again – a rota of household tasks, repeated daily. The pace of our lives has quickened. There are pauses, of course, the occasional idle moment. But that's only because *housework can't be stockpiled*. Socks can't be darned before they've got holes in them, dishes can't be washed before they're dirty. But even if we do have an hour or two of actual free time between the midday round of shops–lunch–dishes, and the afternoon round of kids–tea–fights–supper–bedtime, what can we do with that time? It's not long enough or definite enough for us to think of taking a job. It's too short a time even to go out, since home is probably miles from anywhere. As a result this hard-earned respite becomes a time of dreadful boredom, solitude and despair. It's then that you stand back and look at yourself – like a puppet, gesticulating in all directions but not actually moving in any of them. Do you live to work yourself to death, to bleed yourself white day after day, just to give support and sustenance to your husband so that he can sell his labour to pay for the food, clothes and home that you prepare, repair and maintain? You are given moments of rest and holidays with the family for no other reason than to keep you working next day, next month and next year. Your children are with you, in reality, so that they can become a new generation of workers. There are times when women would willingly turn their hands, in myth so tender and loving, into clenched fists.

No, Electrolux doesn't liberate women! Nor does the soap powder which washes whiter. And we, daughters of the Kenwood Chefette and Madame Soleil of the agony column, know what we're talking about. Women won't be liberated until the function of the family in our society is itself destroyed. Among the oppressed classes the family exists to produce the workers of the future and to care for today's workers and keep them in good shape. Our children and our husbands are supposed to turn out as the bourgeoisie want them to. Under capitalism, the bourgeoisie in a sense 'consume' our children and husbands – at least they consume their labour-power. So they require our husbands and children to be physically, intellectually, morally and politically oppressed.

If capitalism could, without jeopardizing its own existence, concentrate workers in large barracks, giving them the bare minimum for survival, and put all their children into orphanages, then maybe the condition of women would be *modified*. It might begin to look a bit more like the condition of men – but would that be liberation? Of course this is an absurd hypothesis, because the fluidity of with and the competition the work force imply that they must reproduce themselves *privately*, everyone having his own independent responsibility to meet the requirements of capitalist society as fully as possible and on all levels. Otherwise they face the threat of being rejected by the production process, and perishing.

No wonder the princes who govern us aren't very keen on discarding this family – from their point of view, it's a necessary machine that has more than proved itself over the years.

3 Collectivization First, then Mechanization

The socialization of housework *necessarily* implies the denial of the economic role of the family, and therefore of its traditional political role. This in turn makes the creation of new institutions to take over family functions like feeding, clothing, educating and relaxation an absolute priority. Destroying the family as an economic and political unit is a challenge to all revolutionaries, but ensuring that the useful functions of the family are still carried out is another matter altogether. Kollontai, a leading Bolshevik in the twenties, advocated (among other measures) the creation of a corps of workers who would take over the household chores that enslaved women. But who would then free these liberators from the drudgery? Kollontai has nothing to say about that. To abolish oppressive division of labour by the introduction of a new division of labour solves nothing. 'The individual household has passed its zenith. It is being replaced more and more by collective housekeeping. The working woman will sooner or later need to take care of her own dwelling no longer; in the communist society of tomorrow this work will be carried on by a special category of working women who will do nothing else.' [1] Do women protest at their household confinement? Don't they want to be the semi-skilled workers of the home any more? No matter! We'll create a specialized corps of workers (Kollontai says *women* workers!) who will do not only their own housework, but everyone else's as well. What a victory!

Socialism doesn't consist of higher pay for boring jobs, or of handing over the boring jobs to a small section of the workforce. Socialism is about the complete elimination of the repetitive and absurd aspect of work. And if it hasn't yet been eliminated in a certain kind of work, the answer isn't to hand over that work to a single battalion. The work should instead be distributed as widely as possible, so that, with everyone doing his or her bit, no one is enslaved.

IMAGES AND DISCUSSIONS ON THE CHINESE ROAD

It was a cool Thursday in December when we filmed the big weekly cleanup at the Shanghai workers' housing estate. Children of all ages, kitted out with brooms and dustpans, are sweeping paths, picking up leaves and litter (though there is very little litter because the Chinese are now a 'socially responsible' people). Two teams of retired workers are washing down staircases, other people are cle cleaning windows, while little groups potter about here and there, mending a damaged door or a leaking fountain. The whole scene is extraordinarily lively and busy. Some people are taking advantage of the situation to continue a discussion with their neighbours or to teach one another new songs. This is unpaid work; it's voluntary and collective. No one is taken to court for refusing to participate. And yet if someone systematically avoids doing the work, or does it 'just to get it over with', he or she will always be confronted by a group of youngsters who will argue and criticize until they convince him or her of the importance of collective, voluntary work.

A discussion in Xiao Wang

The Chinese way gives priority to the struggle against the traditional division of labour, without waiting for any preliminary technological progress. The narrow village lanes in the Xiao Wang people's commune zigzag towards a square where new buildings have been constructed – small, low buildings with whitewashed brick walls and slightly upturned roofs, vaguely reminiscent of pagodas. Each door leads to a flat. Each flat has a mud floor and a wooden staircase leading from the kitchen to the bedrooms on the next level. The communal rooms open directly on to the square. On the day we were there people were eating their meals on their doorsteps and chatting to one another. A wide-brimmed straw hat was hanging on one white wall, a dark wooden flour sifter on another. The atmosphere was simple and warm.

There was hardly any evidence that work here was mechanized. As in most villages, there was electricity in all the houses, but no running water and no mains drainage. A smiling young woman offered us tea in her house. Neighbours dropped in, greeted us with a nod and joined the conversation. Our questions were all concerned with the central difficulty of solving the problem of housework in conditions of such rudimentary comfort. The girl told us: 'We must try to develop mechanization in the area of domestic work. The peasants in this district are working on it, but we mustn't wait until this mechanization has been achieved to release women from their traditional duties. Up to fifteen years ago, there was no electricity, no mechanical aids to housework and no crèches. In order to create farming co-operatives, the peasants found ways of compensating for their lack of means. Small children were taken to the fields, where the older children looked after them while copying characters to help them to learn to write. The old people would take charge of collective services for the village, running the clothing repair workshops and the laundry, for example. At harvest time they would prepare the communal meals. This custom has survived and to this day, when there is a big job to be done, communal meals are still prepared.

Housework is shared equally among all members of the family, so that everyone – husband, wife, grandparents and children – participates in running the house. When a man not only does the washing-up but prepares meals, scrubs the floor, sews on buttons, dresses the youngest child's cuts and bruises, and does all that regularly *throughout* the week, not just on Sundays, he is no longer a husband in the accepted sense of the word.

The dramatic change in the status of the village women has its roots in the struggle for the socialization of the land. It was during this struggle, as we have seen, that the women gained recognition as a political force. It's an easy matter to demand servility from a submissive, silent wife who has no experience of the world beyond her limited family horizons. Try refusing to scrub the floor if your wife has spoken up before the entire village, if she has had the courage to stand up to wealthy peasants, if she has struggled to close the ranks of the peasants, if she has organized teams of women who tomorrow will join the men in irrigating the fields! Refusing to scrub the floors if your wife has enjoyed the support and applause of a whole village is another matter altogether!

The emergence of women as a political force brought with it a change in their household status. And the Xiao Wang women have ways of convincing a recalcitrant man that this change has come. As a first step, his wife will try to persuade him by discussing the issues. If that fails she will readily call on the whole family for support. If that has no effect, the women's committee of the village will visit him *en masse* and insist, politely but firmly, that he must remember the difference between socialism and feudalism. In the unlikely event of the man still clinging stubbornly to his attitudes after all this, the whole village may support the woman with a campaign of mass criticism – and, as a last resort, she can always divorce him.

The young woman concluded: 'It was mainly taking part in the class struggle that made us understand the origins of our enslavement, and enabled us to change our situation as women.'

We had met many women veterans of the revolution before this visit, and had listened to their stories. These women all seemed to suggest the truth that this peasant woman had now spelled out. Because Chinese women rose against feudalism and against the class enemy, they became more aware of their specific oppression. Those peasant women who had taken part in the struggle against the Japanese invasion saw the necessity of destroying the old family structure before victory could be achieved. Feudal traditions had barred women from working in the fields and denied them any possibility of economic independence in the social system as it then was. During the war against Japan many of the able-bodied men left the fields to enrol in the People's Army. If women had not taken over agricultural production in the liberated areas, the people in those areas could not have survived and become self-sufficient. But that takeover was itself a massive blow against feudalism, and without it the revolution would have failed. It's often in the struggle for the recognition of their *right to make the revolution* that women will gauge the extent of their specific oppression. In the same way, the mass of peasant women who fought for the socialization of agriculture gained essential *social* experience in this struggle, and therefore widened their horizons. They are bound to see traditional housework even more clearly as a tight and restricting yoke standing in total opposition to the revolutionary role that they want to play and actually are playing. We were often told of working-class or peasant women who would be criticized by husband or family for wanting to go out to work. 'It's ludicrous, there's plenty of money coming in, why on earth do you want to go out to work?' 'To make the revolution!'

The first necessary step towards the development of a clear idea of our particular oppression is not always obvious. Why was it that in capitalist countries a large minority of women had to go into industry, or other areas of social involvement, before women's movements could begin? It was doubtless because the experience of social labour suddenly enlarged the female perspective, which had until then been confined to the insoluble problem of the family. For the first time ever, a woman's situation did not appear to be the inescapable will of God, but the inevitable consequence of an inhuman social structure, transforming men into production-machines, and women into a maintenance crew for these machines. As a result of their entry into social production, women learnt who was responsible and whose interests were really served by their domestic slavery. It was a lesson they could never forget.

A REVEALING PARALLEL BETWEEN THE SOCIALIZATION OF HOUSEWORK AND THE SOCIALIZATION OF AGRICULTURE

We found again and again that socialization – in the sense of a transformation of relations between people – is not conceived by the Chinese as a stage which follows the development of mechanization.

The two are undertaken together and progress together. We saw how this is happening with the women workers in small neighbourhood factories like Chao Yan. The same approach applies equally to housework. 'We mustn't wait until mechanization has developed before starting on socialization,' a young woman explained to us. This brought to mind what Trotsky had said while he was still one of the leaders of the Soviet Union: 'We need socialist accumulation; *only* under this condition will we be able to liberate the family [and therefore women] from all the functions and cares which now oppress and destroy it.' [2] This idea came to be used as the standard justification for not finding the necessary solution to the problem of housework. Meanwhile women continued to do their two jobs a day and to suffer more or less overt contempt from society, precisely because they were still 'housewives'. In fact this amounted to making the emancipation of women dependent on the technical progress of an industry in which they played particularly minor roles, and not at all on their own labour. Basically it fell to technicians to liberate or not to liberate women from domestic oppression.

Trotsky's position on this was hardly unique. At that time such sanctification of economic development through technology was common all over the Soviet Union and in all spheres. Stalin viewed the problem of agriculture, for example, in much the same way. The argument goes like this: the socialization of agriculture depends on mechanization, which depends on the building of tractors, which depends on the development of heavy industry. Meanwhile the peasantry, the mass of small landowners who aspire only to become kulaks, must be regarded with the greatest suspicion. Peasant crops can be requisitioned, and peasant labour diverted to keep industry going. And when the day of the long-awaited leap forward in productive forces finally arrives, tractors are simply brought to the fields chosen by decree to become state property or *Kolkhoz* (collective farm) property, without further ado. Peasants become farm labourers overnight and collectivization is achieved.

China's first step towards collectivization was to set up simple agricultural co-operatives. This preceded mechanization. A cart, often hand-drawn, was a highly valued production tool. Before all else, the human workforce, its energy and enthusiasm, was socialized. Mechanization has developed from this basis and its progress is evident. We saw a little remote-controlled cultivator ploughing the side of a very steep hill, narrowly terraced like a staircase. When the cultivator reached the end of one terrace it would rear up almost vertically, go down one step and plough the lower level in the opposite direction. A few dozen meters above it, a peasant leaning against a tree operated the machine from a simple control box.

When the ideological aspect of the revolution, the transformation of work relationships and political consciousness are given their proper priority, technological progress is sure to correspond to the needs of the masses, and to help to put socialism into practice.

Chen Yung Kuei, the peasant leader of the Tachai commune and a well-known figure in China, writes about the experience of his brigade:

Only by following Chairman Mao's teaching of using the ideological revolutionisation to lead agricultural mechanisation forward can we guarantee that mechanisation will advance along the socialist road... Some people think it [mechanisation] is aimed only at reducing labour intensity and providing more leisure, and they do not understand that mechanisation is the Party's fundamental line in the rural areas for adhering to socialism and defeating capitalism. Others regard agricultural mechanisation as an ordinary measure to save labour and increase production. They fail to see it from a higher level and regard it as a measure which consolidates the worker peasant alliance, promotes socialist industrialisation and reduces the differences between workers and peasants. They also do not understand that unless we implement Chairman Mao's revolutionary line mechanisation will not necessarily bring about socialism and it may even lead to capitalism... *Therefore* to carry out farm mechanisation it is necessary to firmly grasp ideological revolutionisation and always carry out as a matter of primary importance the raising of the masses' ideological level and their understanding between the two lines. Otherwise, farm mechanisation will go astray . . . Mechanisation is by no means merely a technical problem.[3]

The marked similarity in attitudes towards agricultural work and housework (both in China and in the Soviet Union, though in very different ways) can be readily explained. Both agriculture and housework require the transformation into a social industry of a work process based on the family unit and strongly tied to small holdings of private property — the peasant's plot or the housewife's house. It's clear that, as Mao has said, this transformation can't be achieved without those concerned freely expressing their desire for it. But even given that desire, the transformation is bound to fail where archaic means of production are destroyed only to be replaced by structures in which the masses are denied all power.

Many of the poor peasants who had willingly accepted the collectivization of the land and the creation of the *kolkhoz* in the Soviet Union joined the opposition to the Soviet regime when they realized that they would have no say in the running of their collective farm. Technicians and *apparatchiks*, denying the peasants any of their specialized knowledge, made all the important decisions about what was to be produced, how, when and in what quantity — with catastrophic results for agricultural production.

The close similarity between the problems presented by small agrarian property and those presented by domestic work enabled Chinese women to make the breakthrough which allowed them to criticize vigorously the Liuist policy of restoring capitalism in rural areas. In my opinion this is one of the fundamental reason why women could be in the vanguard in the sort of struggles we had been told of in Xiao Wang — where the connection between the struggles and the specific oppression of women might not have been immediately discernible.

Liu Shao-chi's policy made explicit the following aims: setting up a free market where prices would be fixed according to capitalist laws of supply and demand; extending individual plots (which could of course be inherited); creating individual enterprises fully responsible for their own profits and losses; and using the family to establish production norms. This policy was called Zhen-Zui-Yi-Bao, an abbreviation for the various measures. (Along with this policy went a call for the 'four freedoms — freedom to practice usury, freedom to hire farmers, freedom to buy and sell land and free enterprise.) Each of the measures can be seen at once in terms of the oppression of women, especially the one that was the *sine qua non* of all the others: *the recognition of the family as a unit of production*, a family with an urge to become wealthy, since it would reap the benefit of its own profits, but threatened by ruin since it would equally bear the responsibility for its own losses.

Liu Shao-chi proposed exactly this sort of family life, with its burden of feminine 'curses': the duty of motherhood – to produce heirs who will increase the workforce; the slavery of housework – so that the husband can devote all his energy to farming; the prison of the home; the degradation of being an eternally submissive 'minor'; the race to catch a husband; the right to keep her opinions to herself. This was the 'paradise' promised by the 'four freedoms'. This is no doubt one of the root causes of women's opposition to Liu. But in this case, too, opposition couldn't crystallize and strengthen until the women had another solution or were able to envisage the possibility of another solution. Such knowledge or vision allowed them to relegate the 'blessings' of private property to the status of museum pieces.

THE REVOLUTION IN TOWN-PLANNING

The Soviet experience

During the years following the revolution in the Soviet Union an intense debate took place among architects: 1 October was the foundation-stone of a new world in which everything still needed to be done. Soviet Russia was a town-planner's dream. The problem, of course, was not how to build cosy semis for the new world, but how to collectivize housing. There were bitter clashes between differing schools of thought. One of them, following Sabsovich, typified the search for new approaches. Their theory was simple: material structures, acting as 'social condensers' would help to build up new relationships between people. It was, therefore, necessary to build to fit this function. The most extreme project of these town-planners was to construct communal buildings designed for several thousand inhabitants, consisting of units divided into three parts. One part was to be reserved for children, another for men and the third for women. Heated corridors would connect the different sections. Kuzmin had calculated to the nearest second how long each of the necessary actions of daily life should take – all of them at breakneck speed! Daily life was organized as if the people were living in the archetypal capitalist factory: rationalized, standardized, Taylorized and stupefying. In reality, this sort of thinking revealed a thorough understanding of the family's traditional role in maintaining and reproducing the workforce, and the only advance it represented was that the State should take over this formerly individual function. [4]

The main reason for abolishing women's domestic work was the need for profit. Sabsovich stated in one of his pamphlets that thirty-six million work-hours were spent daily on preparing family meals. He commented: 'It would take only six million hours to do the same work in kitchens-cum-factories, which would then deliver the hot meal in thermos-flasks to the various canteens.' [5] We have nothing against collective kitchens or canteens. Welcome as they are, it is none the less particularly distressing when the pressure to abolish women's domestic burdens arises only from a concern with profitability. At least Soviet women could be thankful that technological means were available to do domestic work faster than they could. Otherwise plenty of feminists would doubtless have advised them to stay at home.

The 'concentration camp' dreams of the town-planners were to have a strange fate. Kopp reports: 'Supercollectivization was a utopia, even a dangerous utopia. It went against the instincts of the population, and, in fact, every communal house built during that period was rapidly converted (by means sometimes rough and ready) into something that more closely resembled a home, in the usual sense of the word.' [6] This wasn't because the Soviet people opposed collective services in principle – indeed the local and national press of the time was full of demands from all over the place for more crèches, restaurants and youth centres – but because of the rationale behind the homes they had been forced to live in. The buildings were an artificial and authoritarian attempt to revolutionize social relations outside any mass initiative, rather than frameworks for the expression of new social relations arising from the revolution in production and the struggle of the people. The social relations imagined by bureaucratic planners had nothing to do with the reality of revolutionary change and revealed great contempt for the masses, who were seen as malleable dough which had merely to be poured into a mould to take on the desired shape.

And what was the outcome of the great debate on housing which lasted several years? Vast dormitory-towns, Stalin-allee style, exactly like the huge Municipal workers' estates familiar to us in the West. And those who were able to live there were the lucky ones, because the housing crisis has never been solved and millions of people have continued to survive as best they can in wooden shacks, deserted warehouses or, as Yvon mentions,[7] in the Moscow underground while it was still under construction. The bureaucratic housing projects had other shortcomings: they couldn't be built without modern materials like concrete, glass and steel, and modern techniques, such as the systematic use of cranes. Many of the planned buildings simply couldn't be built in prewar Russia. Some could be realized only as avant-garde experiments, reserved for a minority. The housing projects could in no way present a realistic solution to the problems of the millions of homeless and badly housed people.

China's choice

Anyone who expects to find a new architecture in China, a new world translated into stone, will probably be very disappointed at first. On the day we arrived we saw many recently built blocks of flats from the bus taking us the 30 kilometers from the airport to Peking. These blocks were four or five storeys high and made out of rough, uncovered bricks, which made them look strangely unfinished to us. It hadn't rained in Peking for a long time and in the midday sun the bare earth pavements and the walls of the houses looked as though they'd been painted a matching burnt-sand colour. Against this background the numerous trees appeared as large green patches and their cool shade shimmered in the light. There was no sign of new architectural forms.

The first priority after the liberation was to give everyone a roof over his head. And that was no easy matter in a country where millions of peasants owned nothing but the rags on their own backs (sometimes not even that since two peasants would often take turns wearing a single sackcloth coat – as an elderly worker, whose face bore the marks of past hardships, was telling the pupils in a Nanking primary school we visited) and it must be remembered, too, that China had just emerged from thirty years of war which had left behind a, trail of ruin and destruction.

At the time of the agrarian reforms all existing houses were divided into sections and distributed as a matter of course to the homeless. William Hinton gives a very precise and detailed account of this.[8] We saw some of the rural manor houses which had formerly belonged to wealthy landowners and were now lived in by several households (quite often related). Such redistribution of property also took place in the cities. Houses which had belonged to class enemies were naturally requisitioned, and the remnants of the national bourgeoisie were also forced to give up rooms to workers. Of course these were extreme measures designed to cope with an emergency. The real need was for more buildings. However this period did have some lasting and positive effects. Families who lived together had to share kitchens, lavatories and water supplies, and this helped to collectivize household tasks, or at least to undermine the mystification of them as private tasks.

The next problem was whether it was wiser to postpone the building of large blocks of flats until modern materials were available (which could mean a long wait, given the low level of industrial development at the time of the liberation), or to start immediately on building a large number of small units by *mobilizing the people*. Considerable aid from the Soviet Union made it possible to rebuild quite a few large blocks, especially public buildings like assembly halls, hospitals, universities and department stores. But the problem was really solved by adopting the second alternative. To build brick houses with trowels requires no great technological development, only a sufficient quantity of bricks and mortar. The brick kilns were working to full capacity, but even that wasn't enough, so everyone took to firing bricks in their spare time.

In the Ling district we saw children packing a kind of damp earth into iron moulds which looked just like gadgets for making toasted sandwiches, and placing the moulds in rows by the roadside to dry in the sun. A little further on a peasant was putting them into an oven like buns. Countless blocks of houses have been built in this way, with next to no investment, and relying on the skill and ingenuity of the masses. These housing blocks usually have one shared kitchen to every two or three flats. There are mains supplies of electricity and water and town gas in the kitchens.

As construction costs are low, so are rents: a flat costs, on average, 5 yuans a month (the average worker's wage is 70 yuans a month). Water, gas, electricity, basic furniture, maintenance and repairs (such as painting and replacement of window-panes) are all included in the rent.

4 The Example of Taching

THE POLITICS OF CONSTRUCTION IN CHINA

The Taching oilfield, the largest in China, was pasture only ten years ago. Today it is peopled by over forty thousand labourers, technicians and their families. First of all I must point out that we weren't able to visit Taching; I believe that, with the exception of Anna Louise Strong,[1] no foreigner has ever visited it. But it's important to mention it here because Taching is the Tachai of industry, i.e., an avant-garde production unit which serves as a model for the whole of China. If you really want to understand the Chinese revolution you must know about not only the average level of development, but also the advanced experiments which suggest the ways in which the society might progress. And although it is relatively well documented, many people interested in China still know too little about the Taching experiment.

Construction policy in China is not only to mobilize the masses to compensate for the lack of technological development but also, and more fundamentally, to forge a close link between the problems of urban life and the problems of society as a whole. But this link could be forged only if workers and peasants were admitted to the field of architecture, which was formerly the province of specialists. Only the mass of workers and peasants could be trusted to orient the building industry towards the needs of the people and of the revolution.

Taching is a typical example. When the first workers and technicians arrived there in 1959 they found only shepherds' mud huts to live in. Since there were no towns and very few villages almost everything had to be started from scratch. With the shepherds' help, the Taching pioneers used the traditional materials and techniques of the region to build new cobwork houses (their insulating properties are such that they are cool in summer and warm in winter). Some people thought that these houses should be only temporary dwellings, and that some grandiose scheme, on a par with the oilfields themselves, should eventually be put into effect. They argued that no one could seriously expect the cream of China's labourers and technicians — some of the most advanced in the world — to live in mud huts like shepherds. Such a situation was so ridiculous as to be inconceivable. A group of specialists suggested that a vast oil city should be built, concentrating all the accommodation and services necessary for the workers and their families' daily needs.

The great majority of the Taching population strongly opposed the project on several grounds. The oil wells were scattered over a radius of about 20 kilometers. One giant oil city would have introduced the problem of time wasted in travelling to and from work, when the point was to keep travelling time to a minimum. The project would have necessitated a vast investment while there were cheap materials on the spot which had already proved their value. Finally, and above all, such a city would widen the gap between town and country instead of closing it. If the oil people lived in their own special city they would be cut off from the peasants and shepherds in the area. That would be tantamount to ignoring the revolutionary alliance between workers and peasants. And then, what would the Taching workers eat? Surely not oil? Settling the Taching workers in a city would merely confirm their total dependence on food imports from the agricultural regions, and actually create the economic imbalance typical of capitalism.

For all those reasons, the 'grandiose scheme' was rejected. The workers elected an 'architecture committee', made up of architects, labourers, technicians, shepherds, housewives and party cadres, who put forward other proposals. This committee embarked on a searching inquiry. All the people of Taching were asked what they wanted and all the criticisms levelled against the cobwork houses were collected. The committee worked in close association with the peasants, trying to understand better the advantages and disadvantages of traditional houses. Eventually they suggested a new model house in improved cobwork. This new project was then fully discussed by the people, altered again and finally put into practice. Between 1962 and 1966 *a million square meters* of living area were built by this method, which was also used to build crèches, schools, welfare clinics, offices, workshops, shops, cinemas and public buildings. Only the refinery, the central hospital and the Oil Research Institute were built in conventional materials (concrete and steel) because they were too large and too tall to be made from mud.

At the request of the women the houses were planned to accommodate several families (between three and five each). Each house was designed to have communal areas (one large kitchen and a common living room) and private areas, so that each family would still have their own flat. The people insisted that the outside of the houses should look bright and attractive. The lower part of the walls was to be kept dark brown, the colour of rough cobwork, and the upper area was to be painted ochre. Doors and windows, as well as the wooden cornice supporting the thatched roof, would be painted in a bright contrasting colour, usually bright blue.

The houses were sited to facilitate decentralization. The Taching community was divided into several districts, often quite far apart, but in such a way that homes would be near work places. Because the building techniques were simple, the necessary materials were available free. The workers built their own houses with the help of neighbours, and consequently the accommodation was rent-free. The fuller exploitation of oil resources has made available the natural gas contained in the oil. The gas is sent all over China in tankers and is carried to all Taching's houses in special pipes, giving them free heating.

No matter how well they've been planned, houses are only houses, and can't create life where there hasn't been any. The reason why today the districts make up living communities, and Taching as a whole is a model for all China, is that there is, probably for the first time in history, a balance between industry, agriculture, cultural activities and nature. Only mankind could have achieved this: in Taching, however, mankind has been predominantly womankind.

Mother Shui, a new kind of mother courage

Taching's various oil wells, pipelines and refineries take up only a very small proportion of the whole vast area. In 1962 the rest of Taching consisted mostly of extensive pasture land and a considerable amount of fallow land. In the spring of that year, a series of unprecedented natural disasters had resulted in a bad harvest all over China. Grain had to be rationed. Many wives of workers newly settled in Taching decided to take up spades and pick-axes to help to improve their diet. They started tilling the earth to plant vegetable gardens near their homes.

But Mother Shui, a fifty-year-old whose husband and three children worked in the oil wells, wasn't satisfied with that. She thought that oil workers' wives shouldn't be content simply to look after a few vegetable gardens, even if these gardens did belong to everybody; that was only a makeshift solution in view of the temporary difficulties China was going through. Her plan was altogether different. 'The women should transform Taching, an industrial area, into a vast industrial and agricultural complex, and to achieve this, we should set out to conquer the fallow lands.' She convinced four of her women neighbours that she was right.

After consulting the local peasants they chose a few fallow fields about 30 kilometers away from their homes. They had to overcome one immediate problem. At that time there were no crèches or child-minding facilities available and they had young children. 'Never mind. We'll take the children along with us, and decide later how to organize the necessary services.' And so one morning they set out with their five spades, some tinned food, a tent, saucepans, the children and a few kilograms of seed. They pitched their tent in a field half an hour's walk from a village. The first evening a terrible wind got up and they spent the whole night hanging on to the tent. In spite of that, the following morning they started digging in the field. In three days they had dug five mous of land. On the fourth day, at daybreak, they saw about twenty women and thirteen children coming towards them. The newcomers said to Mother Shui, 'We were worried about you the other night during that high wind. We thought, "Those women and children are defying the wind and the cold, all for the good of the community, while we're tucked up in bed in the warm. They're transforming the world, and what they're doing we can do as well." So here we are!' Mother Shui was so happy she was speechless. Very soon the community was organized. One woman looked after the kids while the others dug the earth. They cleared and sowed 16 more mous, which yielded a crop of 1925 kilograms of soya beans. And so Taching's first 'farming brigade' was born.

The following year a village with two hundred houses was built on the brigade's work site. Mother Shui set out to clear more new land, taking with her about a hundred women. This time the women took time to organize themselves. They built collective cobwork houses (like those described above) for themselves and the families who had followed. Their first job was to organize a crèche and a school. The problem of the crèche was easily solved. They collected playpens and cots in one of the cobwork houses, fixed up a lovely garden area and placed the children in the care of volunteer grandfathers and grandmothers. A primary-school teacher set up the school with the help of other women. Some classes, such as those on the history of the revolution, were taught by men and women who had taken part in the great struggles of the past but were not qualified teachers. The women also insisted that boys as well as girls should get some basic training in collective housework. They set up sewing and shoe-repair classes. A larger workforce was available for farm labour and that year the first crop was harvested from an area of over 150 hectares.

The inventiveness of the Taching women didn't stop there. They organized a people's canteen, collective workshops for household tasks, and, with the newly arrived doctors, a decentralized health-care network. (In Taching every village, no matter how small, has a clinic where minor surgery can be performed.) Later on small factories were built to make various useful objects, ranging from radios, shoes, saucepans, furniture and spare parts to machines like grain threshers. Youngsters, old people and students at the Oil Institute were all drawn in by the extraordinary tide of activities the women had set in motion. Even though less than a third of them would have been considered capable of playing an active part at first, all of them, except the sick, wanted to join in the collective work. This may be one of the most obvious indications of the women's achievement – they managed to expand the scope of their activities from their start in food production to the point when men and women were integrated equally into all areas of the collective effort.

A little-known aspect of feminine specificity
Another feature of Taching life deserves attention. Most collective services are free, such as haircutting, meal preparation, cinemas and transport. The clothes shops and shoemenders' charge for the materials used (like cloth, thread and buttons), but the labour is free. The women themselves are

responsible for these things being free. As I pointed out when discussing the development of neighbourhood factories, women didn't go to work to increase their own incomes, but to play a powerful collective economic and political role which, in transforming their specific condition, would transform the lives of everyone else as well. Their aim was to take one more step towards the communist ideal of 'from each according to his ability, to each according to his needs'. When Mother Shui created the very first farm brigade, the women who participated in it adopted the system of wage determination by work points. This system took into account each person's capabilities. The women who earned the most points decided to give part of their own earnings to women who had material difficulties, such as children with delicate health, judging their need to be greater.

Was it pure chance that women were the first to put such egalitarianism into practice? Or could it be that women down the ages have evaluated their work not by the profit they derived from it, since they were never paid, but by the usefulness of their work to their families? Or could it be that women have always had a communistic tendency to give priority to the social utility of their work? Whatever the reason, Anna Louise Strong reached this same conclusion in her discussion of the women of Taching, including Mother Shui, when she wrote:

This unpaid work in Taching is not very different from what women's work has always been. Women have always worked to supplement the family income in occupations that couldn't be *cost-evaluated*. Nor is it very different from the commune of the future, where tasks will be carried out according to each person's abilities and each person will be remunerated according to his or her needs.[2]

We seem to be touching here on what is nowadays called 'multi-faceted feminine specificity'. Mao Tse-tung issued the directive 'Learn in the school of Taching', in which he specifies: '... conditions permitting, the workers must take part in farm labour as is done Taching's oilfields.' This shows that, having studied the Taching women's experiment, the Chinese Communist Party fully understood the importance it had for the future of the economy and for the progress of communism. Taching is a model because the new form of social organization there integrates town and country by combining the advantages of both. This can be achieved only if all areas of production are collectivized, especially domestic production — that is to say the condition of women must be transformed.

THE ORGANIZATION OF DOMESTIC SERVICES ON A SHANGHAI HOUSING-ESTATE

In urban neighbourhoods as well as in the villages, the 'people's restaurant' is often the most important communal building, and usually the oldest one, because the provision of meals is generally the first domestic task to be collectivized. Taking away from women sole responsibility for meals is an obvious and important step towards liberating them from housework.

Equally significant factors in the setting-up of communal restaurants are the clearly recognizable public usefulness of such establishments, and the fact that all you need is a few large halls.

After visiting a textile factory in Peking we were taken to the restaurant on a housing-estate near the factory. (The factory also had its own canteen, which was open to the workers, their families and friends.) This restaurant was a large high-ceilinged room. When meals were over it became the district's entertainment centre, where people would give performances after their day's work. It was midday and the chopsticks clinked on the crockery. The diners in the restaurant were commenting noisily on a radio news broadcast while they ate. Outside, the squeaky voice of a little girl mingled with the sounds of metalworking in a neighbouring workshop, but once through the door, we were cut off from these street noises. A couple who worked nearby were having a meal with their two daughters. A little old lady was chatting with the young people at her table. A dozen children, between six and eight years old, were eating quietly by themselves. In one corner long serving hatches separated the dining area from the kitchen. People queued there to buy their meals, then went to eat them at one of the long tables in the hall. Some people would buy food to take home in metal containers and eat it with their families. Next to us two tiny children, whose chins barely reached the edge of the serving-hatch, asked for something to eat. The waitress spoke kindly to them and handed them plates, which they took to a table where a man had been eating alone. He smiled at them, and pushed a bowl aside to make room for them. The children started talking to him. He listened attentively, nodding his head, and helped the youngest remove the skin from his fish. Their meal over, the children picked up the man's dishes along with their own bowls and chopsticks and took them to another serving-hatch. The man thanked them and they ran out to the yard, back to their games and the light. They weren't his children, nor were they related to him. They hadn't been deserted, they were simply eating by themselves. And naturally, anyone older than them would have felt a responsibility to keep an eye on them as if they were his or her own children.

Restaurants, we were told, are open every day and for every meal. The restaurant also provides full 'mess-tins' to take away, for anyone who has to travel, for his or her work, or for any other reason. The running of restaurants is generally co-ordinated under the triple direction of the cooks, the consumers and the administrators of the city's other collective services. Restaurants have often been organized by the former housewives of the district and they still look after the day-to-day running of them. Because as there are collective kitchens all over the country the importance of private kitchens has been considerably diminished. In any case, since household kitchens are usually shared by two or three families, they can no longer be described as private. In the houses on this estate there was one kitchen to each floor — one for every two flats. The cooking utensils were used communally and frequently the families had arranged to take turns cooking for everybody. On the day of our visit a grandfather and his granddaughter were preparing a meal for two families.

Other collective services like those set up in Taching were open to us for lengthy visits, especially in Shanghai. Their main feature is that women have set them up themselves: This means that both their organization and their development are closely bound up with the women's will to destroy the privatized, familial aspect of household tasks.

In the midst of groups of multi-storey houses stood small newly built single-storey buildings round which the daily life of the district revolved. Their doors were open on to the streets, and you could hear the noise of machines and conversation. People were going in and out, carrying packages. In front of one such building a bicycle with a sidecar stopped for the driver to deliver quite a few rolls of fabric. Clothes were being cleaned and mended in this workshop. The workers would go round the flats in the morning and collect anything that needed mending – torn shirts, socks with holes, trousers that had come unstitched, anything with buttons missing or frayed collars, slippers to mend, clothes to take in or up. Back in the workshop they set to work. One man was sewing on a patch, then a button; a woman was stitching a hem; two sewing-machines placed face to face were working on something with a large floral pattern of – probably an eiderdown. It often takes a day or less to mend and return all the clothes that come in in the morning. And it costs their owners hardly more than the price of the thread and material.

There are services of this kind for shoe-mending, laundry, ironing, respringing mattresses and making clothes to measure. They have two very important qualities: they are meant to be extensively used by the masses, and are therefore in the heart of the housing-estates (for maximum effectiveness), they are also very cheap. There are also workshops which undertake small repairs on utensils and furniture – mending holes in pans and saucepans, sharpening scissors and knives, fixing a damaged door on a wardrobe or a window that's sticking. There are also cleaning services, which clean flats out regularly and at very low cost, even given a worker's budget.

The teams of workers who run these service workshops have, more often than not, been set up by women, but they don't involve only former housewives. Most importantly, retired workers in good health can continue to perform socially useful activities in these shops. This is one of the ways in which old people are integrated into society. Others, people who are still working, often spend some time in these shops as well. They can put in six hours a day, or sometimes as little as three or four hours. This enables people, in poor health and also youngsters outside school hours, to participate, and gives all workers enough time for extra-mural activities. Sometimes these are 'artistic' activities – such as setting up amateur theatrical groups or choirs. Sometimes people may continue their education or learn a new trade – for example a housewife might train to become a 'barefoot doctor' on her housing-estate.

The introduction of more and better machines into the collective workshops already established is a constant preoccupation of workers and political cadres. The workshops, like any other factory, have small innovation teams, made up of workers and technicians, who try to develop new mechanical processes and to find ways of simplifying the work. In one place they were working to perfect a rapid and economical system for drying clothes. In another they were working on a new machine to comb out the stuffing for mattresses. Somewhere else the team is trying to make a small darning-machine. All these teams are linked to consumer-goods factories to study jointly different ways of meeting the needs of the people. While mechanization is not a necessary precondition for the socialization of productive work, it is a vital means of maintaining it.

The prices for the collective services are very low, so the workers are paid out of the municipal funds for their area. The State will subsidize these wages if necessary, but where the municipality is rich enough it alone pays the wages. These are relatively low in the service workshops (about 30 yuans a month), but the working day is often much shorter than in other kinds of factories, and these workers are entitled to free medical treatment, like all other groups.

5 Domestic Production Demystified

While collective workshops are changing the character of the districts, they are also and more profoundly altering the relationships among the people of the districts – first and foremost the relationships that women are involved in. Increasing collectization of housework has made it more and more obvious that the idea of housework as a family-based activity is only a product of a particular (and temporary) social organization that requires individual families to bear the brunt of the responsibility for household work, which has always been just another kind of production. When you've shared the task of darning a whole community's socks with a group of other men and women, you begin to understand why such work was previously servile and inglorious. It was universally scorned and we women were enslaved by it because its useful and necessary character was not *socially* recognized. The attitudes of the old Chinese society to many jobs persist in the West. All manual work is held in contempt, and so, by association, are all those who do it. But such contemptuousness reaches its most extreme and purest form when the work that is done is to maintain house and family.

In the West housework isn't just scorned – it's actually negated. Women, we are told, don't work, they only 'keep themselves occupied'. One of the essential qualities of the Chinese housework collectives is the instructive role they play *vis-à-vis* young people and men. Their very existence has made tangible and inescapable what women in the West have rightly called 'invisible work'. The fact that Chinese men and young people can no longer ignore housework and, indeed, recognize its importance is evidenced by the level of their voluntary spare-time participation in workshop activities and in the collective building of new workshops.

Collectivization has reestablished housework as socially useful labour and, by the same token, those responsible for it have become full citizens as well. Socialization transforms and enriches the lives of former housewives. The district teams, organized and functioning just like any other production unit, participate fully in every area of political life. They carry on debates on the international situation and discussions on government policy, the major issues concerned with the building of socialism and the role of women in the revolution. There is no aspect of Chinese society from which former housewives can be excluded.

Recently the study of Marxism-Leninism has engendered a widespread and powerful movement. Housewives in their fifties, who had had hardly any education, told us, not without pride, that they were currently studying *Materialism and Empirio-criticism* – hardly Lenin's most accessible work.

The teams are also the prime movers in neighbourhood cultural life. China is full of amateur theatre groups, many of them started by former housewives. They put on shows for local people, perform in factories for other workers or act as hosts in their own neighbourhoods to visiting amateur troupes, who may come many miles to perform in a play or in one of the acrobatic displays that the Chinese love so much.

TRADE: A NEW PUBLIC SERVICE

The transformation of retail trade has been a very important factor in freeing women from the burdens of domesticity. Small-scale trade was not abolished after the liberation. Small shopkeepers and traders were asked to regroup into distribution co-operatives, which gradually came under the ownership and control of the collectives – just as had happened with peasants and artisans. Former shopkeepers continued working in their shops, the only obvious difference being that the State now fixed the retail price of goods. Nowadays, of course, there are state department stores with different counters handling a number of different commercial items. But small local shops and travelling markets – all forms of decentralized trading, in fact – have also been developed. These help to maintain close links with consumers. Prices are kept the same in local shops as in the large department stores, and local shops sell all the daily necessities. The Cultural Revolution brought new changes in its wake. The accent is now on the link between production and distribution, and it's up to the sales assistants to match up consumer needs and factory production. They visit their customers regularly to ask their views. Are they satisfied with the quality of such and such a product? Does it work well? Is it easy to use? Is it cheap enough? What are its faults? Have they got any suggestions? The sales assistants take this information to the various production units concerned and together they investigate ways of better satisfying the people's needs. Once a year every sales assistant spends about a month training at the factories where the goods he or she sells are manufactured. This facilitates close political links through China between factory workers, peasants and 'trade workers' (as the Chinese call them). It also helps sales assistants to understand the amount and nature of the labour involved in producing the goods they handle everyday. A young salesman told us that after working in an agricultural commune he realized exactly how valuable the vegetables he sold were. From then on he took special care to keep them fresh, handling them with extra care and even devising a system of ventilated trays to protect them from the damp. He explained that since he had seen how the peasants had to struggle against drought and floods, working hard and selflessly to provide good-quality food for the people, he felt it his duty to ensure that nothing was wasted and that the food stayed fresh. He said that quality, economy and dedication were the lessons he had learnt from his peasant co-workers.

A good knowledge of the goods you are selling also helps in repairing them.

Selling and repair work are therefore increasingly becoming two aspects of a single job. The attitude of one young woman who sold alarm clocks in a department store is typical of the new sales assistants. She felt that she was failing in her work if she knew nothing about the clocks except their prices, so she made a tremendous effort to find out about how they worked, having spent some time working in the factory that made them. Now she never sells an alarm clock without insisting that if it stops as a result of an accident or a manufacturing fault, she will personally repair it. If customers offer to pay her for her repair work, she simply replies that, as a 'saleswoman of the new society', repairs are part of the work for which she is already paid. She comments: 'Before, I didn't know anything about mechanics and this prevented me from serving the people as I wanted to. Now I use my knowledge to serve them better; it's perfectly natural.'

A change in trading which aims to bring consumers and traders closer will obviously play a part in changing the condition of women. The Chinese have avoided the western supermarket model. 'Corner-shop' trading is closer to the Chinese ideal – and such local shops have become genuine public services, unlike the pseudo-service of the supermarket, where minor price reductions are more than offset by the travel and storage costs introduced as a necessary consequence of the super-market/hypermarket system.

A different conception of medicine and its consequences for women

Decentralization of the health service throughout China has the added advantage of releasing women from time-consuming nursing duties, which they are still expected to perform in the West. A Chinese mother no longer has sole responsibility for looking after the health of all her family; nor is she landed with the burden of nursing sick children at home. For one thing, all work places have doctors or worker-doctors (workers trained by doctors while they practise) who take charge of first-aid, and, more importantly, of preventive care. The principles of medicine and nursing are taught in school. Groups of children will wage war on insects in summer. They will also go down a street advising old people to stop their habit of spitting on the ground, or asking people with colds not to go out without protective masks. They know how to treat one another and take great care to follow medical prescriptions. They can also make simple diagnoses, of colds, tonsillitis and stomach upsets, for instance, and can often give first-aid in emergencies. They have some knowledge of acupuncture and use it to cure minor ailments.

In every building complex on the Shanghai housing-estates there is a medical unit. Two or three of the residents, usually former housewives, have been trained by doctors in all the standard diagnoses and treatments. They keep in constant touch with the medical staff of the welfare centres responsible for health care on the housing-estate, and they are in charge of convalescents and people whose illnesses do not require hospitalization. These health workers also make sure that the sick rest as much as possible, bringing them meals, helping them to wash as well as taking the initiative in informing the various district committees that Comrade So-and-so has a broken leg, that they must visit her, bring her reading matter, help her in this or that job – and all without any fuss. No one in China can imagine a situation, so common in the West – and so shocking – where a person is left alone to cope with illness. To get to this stage, all sectors of society had to take an interest in the problems of medical care, so that the practice of medicine could gradually involve the whole population.

Co-operation in the family
It seems to me that there are two aspects to the transformation of housework in China. The first, of which I have given many examples, consists of socializing, regrouping and organizing the work in various ways outside the family structure. It's mainly because of this process of socialization that housework is being progressively eliminated. On the other hand, to make certain tasks the responsibility of some extra-familial administration would actually be harmful to the liberation of housewives. I raise this second point precisely because bureaucracy sees women's liberation as an aspect of the drive to increase productivity through the centralization of production. This stems from a comparison between family labour and social labour. In reality, family work is not familial. It is not done *by* the family, but *for* them – and solely by women. No husband would think of asking his wife to brush his teeth for him, or to dress him, but he finds it natural that she should make his bed, polish his shoes or tidy up after him. This may seem a forced analogy at first sight, but it isn't when you remember that not so long ago the wealthy had chambermaids and valets, whose work was precisely to wash, comb, powder and dress their master or mistress. The Chinese can see no difference between bed-making, clothes-brushing, stitching, sewing, tidying-up and teeth-cleaning. Everyone does these things for himself and considers it the most natural thing in the world. And the reason why it has taken only twenty years for the culture to adapt so completely is that men have been *re-educated*. They have learnt to value housework and no longer contemptuously dismiss it as mere woman's work.

The new women's movement in France also militates in favour of sharing work: 'Of course, first and foremost we insist on the collectivization of housework, but we also want everything which isn't "collectivizable" to be

DOMESTIC PRODUCTION DEMYSTIFIED

shared out equally among us.' In formulating this demand – common sense tells us that it's a legitimate one – the women's movement surely never dreamed that it would provoke an 'armed uprising' among the promoters of 'collective programmes'.

When the French Communist Party remembers women...

It seems that, without realizing it, they had touched a sensitive spot. Just listen to this. After mentioning statistics which show that a worker's wife, doing two jobs a day, one in the factory and the other at home, works eighty to a hundred hours a week, a French Communist Party (PCF) pamphlet continues:

Some clear-sighted people . . . see the remedy to this extra work in equal sharing of household tasks between husband and wife.

Indeed many working women already get considerable help in household tasks from their companion, and we see this as evidence of a new development in a couple's relationship. But expecting to solve the problem of the overburdened working mother merely by an equal distribution of problems and tiredness within the household represents *a limited conception of equality;* for us, this equality must represent a raising of the human condition, making each partner more available to the other and to the children.

'We will make two points:

'1 This 'solution' can only be a palliative at a time when the thorough-going and rapid development of science and technology ought to mean that every household can afford (without having to make sacrifices) the household appliances, which can today mechanize housework. As the statistics show, this is not yet happening . . . 72.5 per cent of French households have a refrigerator, but only 50 per cent have a vacuum cleaner or a washing machine.

2 This 'solution' is a red herring which would free the authorities and the bosses from the obligation to make motherhood easier for the working woman.[1]

There is no need to worry that the PCF may have a 'limited conception of equality' – they simply have no conception of equality at all.

It's obvious that sharing housework won't of itself solve the problem, but it does prepare the way among ordinary people, for the political and ideological conditions which would allow household tasks to be appropriated by grass-roots collectives in a truly egalitarian spirit. Unless such political and ideological foundations are laid, a genuine seizure of power by all workers – and not just by women, even at the head of a battalion of electrical appliances – will be impossible, and we can only fall back on the 'palliatives' suggested by the PCF: the development of individual household appliances with the blessing of the bosses and the State.

Of course egalitarian sharing is not enough, but neither more nor less so than any other partial measure. Only the destruction of capitalist relations of production will do the trick. The outright rejection of any struggle for the egalitarian division of domestic labour, by declaring it to be a 'diversionary manoeuvre', as the PCF has done, is nothing but a superficial and easy pretence of leftism that masks the retrograde point of view criticized by Lenin in certain communists:

> Unfortunately it is still true to say of many of our comrades, 'scratch a Communist and find a Philistine!' Of course, you must scratch a sensitive spot, their mentality as regards woman. Could there be a more damning proof of this than the calm acquiescence of men who see how women grow worn out in the petty, monotonous household work, their strength and time dissipated and wasted, their minds growing narrow and stale, their hearts beating slowly, their will weakened? ... So few men – even among the proletariat – realise how much effort and trouble they could save women, even quite do away with, if they were to *lend a hand in 'woman's work'*. But no, that is contrary to the 'right and dignity of a man'. They want their peace and comfort. The home life of the woman is a daily sacrifice to a thousand unimportant trivialities.[2]

That daily sacrifice of women to a thousand unimportant trivialities is the reality behind the bourgeoisie's mawkish and deceptive homage to 'marvellous motherhood' and the 'irreplaceability' of the mother. Let's hear some more: 'Whether we like it or not, the mother's role is fundamental to the continuation of the species, not only at the time of gestation, but also through all the years it takes to make the child an adult.' Isn't that a very clear statement of the notion of woman as child-rearer and sole bearer of the domestic burden entailed in bringing up children? This hypocritical eulogy of feminine virtues is not an extract from a speech by some Victorian moralist, it is an example of what the PCF thinks is not a limited conception of equality'.[3] They call themselves socialists and, as if to prove it, they label their exaltation of motherhood a 'social function'. 'Motherhood should be considered to be a social function and as such taken into account by society'[4] as if tagging the word 'social' or 'nationalized' or 'real' on to any commodity or product were enough to transform it at a stroke into an authentic socialist product!

Let's take the advice of the ancient Chinese poet and 'sample together this strange literature, and together analyse its obscurities'. 'Motherhood should be considered to be a social function and as such taken into account by society.' Doesn't bourgeois society consider motherhood to be a social function even now? The dominant ideology in our society holds that it is natural for women to devote themselves exclusively to home, husband and children, which is just another way of saying that they *do* fulfil an essential function and that this function is recognized. This 'social function' is so deeply rooted in social custom that it 'goes without saying' that women should perform it. What a strange way of thinking about 'social functions' – and what an empty gesture to women to insist that it should be 'taken into account'. Women's own struggle, on the other hand, will bring real progress, by making this function everyone's, not just the housewives' and mothers'.

The bourgeoisie's attempts to avoid a clash between the working mother's domestic duties and her paid work (by rearranging factory hours, for example) show how vital women and the housework they do are. And that's the whole point. Our society aims to reconcile the irreconcilable, to make paid slavery compatible with domestic slavery, to magnify the exploitation of women to the limit by making them work seventy hours a week, half of it at home and half of it 'at work'. And, by a strange coincidence, the PCF also suggests 'special measures' to 'allow the millions of women who perform a *dual social role,* by both pursuing a career and bringing up children, to *reconcile*[5] these two activities in better conditions'. Meanwhile the ruling class sprinkles a few crèches here and there, a dash of family allowances, half a measure of part-time work and so on, and in the background, the PCF whispers in its ear: 'Put a bit more in, put a bit more in . . . !'

Part Three
SOCIALIZING THE MOTHER'S FUNCTION

6 Infancy and Early Childhood

Transforming the function of motherhood is, as we shall see, a gigantic social undertaking. It can be achieved only by overthrowing existing parent–child relationships, destroying parental authority and the myth of adult infallibility. It requires the whole of society to be deeply conscious of the decisive importance of this transformation for the liberation of women and the future of the revolution. The first step must be to relieve mothers of the continuous care of small children – and, of course, there is even less chance than usual of dealing with this problem without the willing participation of women themselves.

CRÈCHES: CHILD CARE OR CARETAKING?

Crèches are by no means unknown in France. Indeed they are becoming more common daily, but there are still far too few of them. The bourgeoisie constantly impedes the development of collective child care for the sake of what it hypocritically calls 'home crèches'. Home crèches are nothing but child-minders – supposedly state-registered nannies who look after several children in their own homes. The government is firmly opposed to crèches' becoming the universal mode of socialized child-rearing. Crèches are too expensive for the State or bosses to run, of course, but the main objection is that they're a bit too collective. In the long run, crèches pose a threat to the power and the structure of the bourgeois family. The child-minding solution, however, provides all the required guarantees. The nuclear family comes out of it strengthened, for the child-minder merely acts as a mother substitute and the *type* of relationship the child is involved in remains essentially familial. Even though the 'family' changes, it's still one woman, one home, one or more children.

The crèche represents considerable progress in structural terms. Crèches set up in capitalist societies are in some ways blueprints for a radical change which can develop fully only under socialism. And yet because their aim is not to promote women's emancipation or to liberate children, the crèches in France today are highly contradictory. That explains why surveys show that the great majority of women who would like their children to go to crèches, or whose children actually are in crèches, admit that they chose this solution only because it was materially impossible for them to look after their children themselves. These women add, without hesitation, that if they could do so, they would rather look after the children themselves.

How are we to understand this ambivalence? It is, to some extent, the result of women's feelings about work in capitalist societies, which I've already gone into. No doubt it also derives in part from the persistent belief that a mother is irreplaceable and that her role is a natural one; that it is a woman's duty to bring up her infant children herself; and that any other kind of child care is acceptable only if it respects and protects the privileged mother–child relationship. In fact, despite appearances, the ideas and values that crèches espouse do not threaten the mother–child relationship under capitalism in any way. Child-rearing methods and content actually aim to preserve and improve this relationship. But women's mistrust of crèches may perhaps be fundamentally correct, after all.

French crèches, at present, are not in any way run by the parents. As with a school, you leave your child at the crèche in the morning, you pick him or her up in the evening, and you have no say over what goes on in between. It is inevitable that crèches seem beyond the pale of experience, like foreign and hostile territory.

It's difficult to accept with a light heart that your children will be subjected from infancy to a discipline designed solely to train them to submit docilely and in fear to authority and its use of favouritism. Since secondary-school pupils have started to speak out and revolutionary teachers have lucidly denounced the role of the school, no one can remain unaware that school is repressive. Perhaps we are less aware of the extent to which repression operates, often covertly, in kindergartens, and even in crèches.

Make them feel guilty and keep them in their place

Women's mistrust of crèches is only strengthened by the fact that children are cared for exclusively by specialists. Everything conspires to blame the mother for handing over her alleged duty (and her child) to the care of strangers, who are then granted all rights and knowledge with respect to the child. How can the mother who has to leave her child with these experts avoid feeling guilty at what she is told is a betrayal of her maternal role? All this only means more confusion for the mother, who is confronted by the virtual disappearance of mothering traditions from contemporary society. The conditions of everyday life in industrial, urbanized countries are such that a couple's first child is, in all probability, the first child they've ever bathed, dressed and fed. Experienced grandmothers are no longer around to show them how. The distressed and guilty mother ('Is it normal that I shouldn't know how to cope?' 'How do others do it?' 'There's something wrong with me, I'm not a good mother, not a real mother' and so on) usually has no one to turn to but those experts in mothering. The surprised, confused mother then discovers that everything she is doing is

INFANCY AND EARLY CHILDHOOD

totally worthless, old-fashioned and even harmful, and that only properly qualified people know what's good for the child and what isn't. Thus she's never given a chance to extract tried and tested methods of child-rearing from accumulated practical experience of women in this area. And, conversely, she is also prevented from struggling against what really is wrong and old-fashioned.

Everyone knows his or her position and keeps to his or her place. The distraught and guilty mother is forced to desert her child, while the qualified nanny, upholding her status as an expert, is obliged to denigrate the parents and condemn the way they're bringing up their children.

The instructresses at the crèche my little girl used to attend insisted that children shouldn't be potty-trained before they were fifteen to eighteen months old. They thought that premature toilet-training would inevitably lead to a relapse later on. They also wanted to avoid those painful scenes with eight-month-old babies sitting haunched over their pots, their bottoms marked with a red circle when they're lifted off. But this decision was taken without consulting the mothers, who felt that they were still competent in this of all areas, and it provoked incessant bickering, the mothers arguing, 'Well, at home she goes on the pot', while the instructresses reply: 'Never mind that, we don't make them go at the crèche.' There's an implicit plea in the mother's argument: 'I know I'm deserting my child, but allow me at least a little control over him. Don't submerge me completely in the expertise I know you have. Leave me some say in my child's development.'

The argument is an expression of the mother's feeling that she, more than anyone else, knows what's best for her child in at least one sphere. The mothers are kept in such complete ignorance of what their children do all day at the crèche and of the most basic aspects of their development that they feel bitter about even this enforced submission to the professional expertise of others, minor though it is.

Our society constantly and inescapably blackmails the mother who hands her child over to others. It remains true to the principle of giving with one hand and taking away with the other. The mother is offered freedom from time-consuming tasks by Heinz and Mothercare, but at the same time she is blamed for not caring for her own child.

A woman's rights and duties are confused in a society which proclaims left, right and centre that no one can truly take the place of the child's mother. In sending her child to a crèche the mother is bound to feel guilty, with only the fact that she 'couldn't really do anything else' as a mitigating plea. Making mothers feel guilty keeps them in a state of submissiveness and ideological dependence, appropriate to the bourgeoisie's ends. Conditioned with such marvellous ingenuity and such subtle repression, mothers become a party to the child-rearing process the bourgeoisie demands. Not only does the mother bring up her child in the way that society requires, but society itself educates the mother through her child.

The child is a means by which pressure is exerted to mould a woman into the required and pre-determined shape of a mother. The child doesn't deliberately oppress his or her mother, it's more complicated than that. The child becomes the symbol and prop for all kinds of dreams, wishes and myths which subject the woman to her 'call to martyrdom'. The child is the continuation of the family line; he or she is the tribute she owes her husband; the hope of a successful and meaningful life that she has never experienced. The child helps her accept the petty and humble existence which goes no further than her own front door. The child is the meaning of her life. But this subordination to her child isn't without its compensations. According to the bourgeois ideology, the mother's sacred duties entitle her to certain moral rights. Everything follows the proper rules of the market. Without knowing it, she forces her child to pay dearly for the nights she spent at his bedside nursing him when he was ill. She needs him to be totally dependent on her. She smothers, mutilates and paralyses him. In order to appease her desire to give herself, she creates in the child an overwhelming need for tenderness. She allows herself to confine her child's life within the boundaries of the love that only her presence can satisfy. Who is the more miserable on the first day of school, the sobbing child or the mother, upset and yet fulfilled by the despair of the panicking child?

In our experience crèches have done nothing to change this reciprocally cruel and repressive behaviour. At least we could have hoped that mothers would be freed from their material servitude! But even from this most basic of angles crèches haven't been a stunning success.

The organizational failings of crèches are well known. They open too late and close too early, which often forces mothers to juggle with their daily routine or make complicated arrangements, so that, for example, the child can be handed from one person to another before the crèche opens. Crèches refuse to look after sick children, forcing mothers to miss work to nurse their child. If the crèche administration was really concerned to meet the needs of all the people, and of women in particular, a few rooms could easily be left aside for sick children. Women will always be reluctant to hand their children over to collective care as long as crèches continue to be more like a left-luggage office for unwieldy parcels. And our crèches are certainly not places where women can find a way to give society the benefit of their ideas and experience; nor can they be a base for women's own fight against mistaken and reactionary ideas, which also stem from the narrow and selfish nuclear family. If the act of handing children over to group care is to stop causing so much heartbreak, it is particularly important for women to feel that there is some other meaning to their lives than having children – in other words, ultimately they must be integrated into society. Only crèches where mothers could embark on the whole spectrum of revolutionary tasks, set up and organized by themselves, could become places where children are truly socialized. This is possible only to the extent that the initiative taken by women implies that children are no longer the be-all and end-all of their lives and that they wish to fulfil their revolutionary potential – which is to say that they challenge their own limitations and question the traditional repression of children.

A Soviet experiment

The Soviet Union of the twenties, starting from the desire to liberate women from the 'bother' of children but failing to grasp the true importance of the issue, reproduced on a large scale the very faults which characterize capitalist state child-rearing. Shortly after the revolution, Lilina Zinoviev declared: 'We must rescue these children from the nefarious influence of family life. In other words, we must nationalise them. They will be taught the ABC's of communism and later become true communists. Our task now is to oblige the mother to give her children to us – to the Soviet State.' [1] This idea was taken up in Kollontai's formulation: 'Children are the State's concern.' She added: 'The social obligation of motherhood consists primarily in producing a healthy and fit-for-life child ... Her second obligation ... is to feed the baby at her own breast. Only after having done this has the woman ... the right to say that her social obligation towards the child is fulfilled.' [2] One can imagine how this programme could trigger a reaction in the people. Besides the insufferable implications of the enforced separation of mothers from children, it is reactionary in its arrogant presumptions about women. As with bourgeois attitudes, women are considered to be good for nothing but producing children – and probably only good for that until some alternative can be found, just as bottle-feeding can effectively eliminate breast-feeding. They are considered to have no claim on a child's upbringing – that is held to be the province of pedagogues. Women are no longer harangued in the traditional formula of 'Back to your stove, woman!' Now it's become: 'Back to your blast furnace, woman!' In both cases it means the same: 'Shut up, you know nothing about child-rearing. You must stick to the role that society has prepared for you and allotted to you. Let society – that is, the State – decide for you what is or isn't the right method.'

It is sad to realize that such reactionary ideas and such contempt for women are still commonplace in several revolutionary organizations which, despite their many differences, have one thing in common: they all dismiss women's political strength, at best considering it in the dim light of unconnected fragments of speeches at the Third International, mouthed without any thought. But it is even more sickening to come up against such 'male chauvinism' from the pen of one of the women who has most influenced the new women's movement, Kate Millett, when she writes: 'The care of children, even from the period when their cognitive powers first emerge, is infinitely better left to the best trained practitioners of both sexes who have chosen it as a *vocation*, rather than to harried and all too frequently unhappy persons with *little time nor taste* for the work of educating minds, however young or beloved.' [3]

THE ORGANISATION AND SOCIAL FUNCTION OF CHINESE CRÈCHES

Chinese crèches are the product of an entirely different way of looking at things: as Lenin's wife, Krupskaya, said, arguing against both the theory that children are their parents' property, and the theory that they are the State's: 'Children belong neither to their parents, nor to the State, but to themselves', since the State is destined to wither away under communism. It is the whole of society and each of its members, and not the State, that has duties to children. We are all responsible for their physical, intellectual, moral and ideological upbringing.

In China there are crèches in work areas as well as in residential areas; the former are specially intended for unweaned babies, whose mothers come and breast-feed them several times a day. Time spent breast-feeding is counted as work time and is therefore not deducted from their wages. These crèches have, in addition, a political value of even greater importance: bringing children to the work areas, where they can be seen by all the workers, is to say: 'Here are the children we have produced together, for whom we are all responsible. Normally you don't see them. You probably imagine that they get fed, washed, dressed and taken care of by some magic trick without anyone having to look after them. Well, wake up, open your eyes! They are here! What are we all going to do about them?' The women's committee of the factory decide that a crèche must be built right here, and that the men and women will put it up for the children after work. And there, too, men are re-educated. There, too, they learn about the many problems involved in child care. The men finally 'recognize' the children, no longer just as their legal responsibility, as men do in the West, but as complete beings. This means that they fulfil a social responsibility to the children's moral, emotional and political welfare, as well as caring for their bodily needs. Undoubtedly the massive influx of men as crèche 'nurses', which is bound to happen very soon, will lead to profound and positive changes in child-rearing itself, as well as in men's ideas.

The district crèches are usually both crèches for weaned babies (who therefore no longer need to be close to their mothers) and kindergartens for children up to six or seven years old. The staff are still mostly women, a large number of them former housewives. We were told that there are special training schools for nursery workers. But it seemed that these schools were being reformed during our trip so we weren't able to visit them. Apart from these schools, great importance is attached to teacher training and to the exchange of national and regional experiences between crèche workers. Frequent surveys conducted by crèche workers in the neighbourhoods, the factories and the countryside also play an important part in the analysis of experiences gained in the crèches and in enabling appropriate adjustments to be made on the advice of the masses.

Running the crèches is the joint responsibility of crèche workers elected by the staff, parents who use the crèche, delegate workers from the factory and retired workers. Some of the women who look after the children have had special medical training.

With this type of arrangement it's easy for the masses to control the socialization of young children. New methods of child-rearing can be worked out collectively, and the crèche is not the province of specialists.

The crèches are open every day on a twenty-four-hour basis, so that parents who wish to can participate in cultural, artistic or political activities after work. This facility is only for infants, or for those who have no older brothers or sisters to help look after them at home. As soon as a child is a little older, at about two, he or she is more likely to go home every evening. It's also possible for parents to take their baby home in the evening, but leave him or her at the crèche when they want to go out. Finally, since a lot of factories operate day and night, parents can leave their baby there at night and have him or her for a few hours during the day.

Factory crèches are free. Those in the residential district are paid for partly by the factory where the parents work, partly by the neighbourhood's collective fund. The parents' share of the cost is very small.

We spent a day with the children in a crèche at a kindergarten in a neighbourhood in Shanghai.

The setting was very simple, with single-storey buildings. There were pot plants beneath the windows and a large playground in front. When we arrived, at about nine in the morning, it was still quite cold in spite of brilliant sunshine. But the kids were outside, wearing little pinafores (boys as well as girls) over several layers of woollies, making them look like round balls. They were waiting for us with a drum, cymbals, tambourines and paper flowers – a row of noisy, singing and very happy children. We split up into four groups of three, to visit the different parts of the crèche. I went with Edith and Danièle into a room where boys and girls aged three or four were seated round small circular tables, having a domestic science lesson. They were learning how to do the washing up. We would never have imagined that a little boy would know how to scour a bowl skilfully with sponge and powder. The young teacher was watching then. While talking to them, she helped one boy who was having a lot of trouble drying up. Now we could imagine these children really taking part in the washing up at home, without the panicking mother's cries of: 'Be careful, you're going to break that glass!', which end up by paralysing them.

Could you imagine little children in our society actually helping their teachers in their work? At the most they are asked to fold their napkins and put them in their holders. All this made Edith and I think about how often we don't let our children do something because they cause more damage helping than their help is really worth. I wonder if my attitude doesn't reveal an underlying wish to prove to my kids that 'mother knows best', that 'you can't manage without her', that they really need me. Edith reminded me of the day during our last holiday when the 'big ones' (nine years old) had decided to prepare breakfast for the younger ones. I had agreed, but I kept on nagging them all the time, saying again and again: 'You're using too much chocolate, don't forget the sugar, the milk isn't hot enough'. I had no confidence in them, so it was hardly surprising that they couldn't stand it, and after a few days resigned themselves to my doing everything for them. Basically, I was proving that I was right.

What took our breath away watching the washing-up 'lesson' wasn't that the smallest children were being asked to do something useful, but that they were doing it so perfectly. It makes you think. Someone took the trouble to show them and to teach them; someone considered the usefulness of that kind of work for very young children, and the children understood it very well. They knew how to do it collectively, *the boys were as involved as the girls* and it was becoming as natural to them as eating and sleeping. These youngsters come to the table knowing that the meal has had to be prepared, that the table has had to be laid and that afterwards the dishes will have to be washed and put away. They are not just hungry, they are responsible. At the end of the day we had a long discussion with the teachers and the older children (all of five years old). They explained to us that they saw the upbringing of the younger ones as a process in two stages, dialectically linked. The first stage consists of teaching them to acquire personal autonomy as quickly and completely as possible: learning to eat by themselves, to wash themselves, to get dressed, to do as much as possible without the help of adults. Then the emphasis is put on collective education: learning to do together things for everyone – making beds, washing up, doing housework and so on. Of course the two stages are closely connected. How can you ask a child to clean other people's shoes when he or she doesn't know how to put his or her own shoes on? If you do it will seem like a punishment.

What is so amazing is that the work of the youngest children is not treated as a pastime (it's not to occupy them) nor even as trivial help to adults – 'Go and fetch me this! Pass me this! Hold this for me!' – which doesn't give them a complete job to carry out from beginning to end, and which really means that they are being treated as semi-skilled workers, made to do things they can't fully grasp, and reduced to carrying out our orders as subordinates. Even for the very young ones the aim must be to give them full responsibility for one or more useful tasks, even if five or six of them take more time to do it at first than a single adult would. *What is at stake isn't the immediate productivity of the work, but what children can learn from it.*

At a people's commune we had previously visited we had noticed the same concern in the crèche to let the youngest children carry out simple tasks on their own, both looking after the crèche and working in the fields with the peasants. There was a vegetable garden cultivated by the teachers and the children up to seven. Everyone worked there, and of course their ages were taken into account: the youngest ones watered, the older ones dug – maybe only a few square meters each – others sowed and yet others

INFANCY AND EARLY CHILDHOOD

weeded or spread the necessary fertilizers.
A good number of the vegetables eaten by the children at the crèche are products of their own labour. At harvest time they organize themselves into small teams and the revolutionary committee of the brigade gives them jobs like gleaning or spreading the grain on the concrete threshing-floor to dry in the sun. There seemed to us to be many different links between the adults of the village and the children. This is not peculiar to the countryside; in the cities, too, the children in the crèches are organized, from the youngest age and without sex distinctions, to do useful little jobs in their neighbourhoods. Children in kindergartens begin to take part in social production from the age of three or four. For example we saw children seated round long low tables, helped by their teachers, folding the little cardboard boxes used to pack the medicines manufactured in a nearby factory. Obviously they don't spend much time doing this each week and their productivity is low, but how proud they are when they set off in close formation, the red flag leading the way, to deliver their products to the factory workers!

Outside these activities, the emphasis for the three to seven-year-olds is on music, dancing, gymnastics and lessons in history and the class struggle. We went to a history lesson for children of five to six in a Shanghai kindergarten. The children sat round the teacher. There were posters on the wall of a little boy of about twelve, in rags and alone in a forest. The teacher told the story of little Chang, the son of poor peasants, during the war against the Japanese. The suffering inflicted by feudal lords and the humiliation suffered by the Chinese people at the hands of the Japanese imperialists make little Chang, whose parents have been murdered by the local tyrant's men, want to join the People's Liberation Army. The young woman stops her story and asks the children what obstacles Chang will meet on his journey. A little girl replies:

'The cold.'

'Quite right,' says the teacher. 'Little Chang will be cold at night. What will he do?'

'Try to find a blanket, or a bag to wrap himself in,' a little boy suggests.

'Build himself a shack in the woods,' suggests another.

'Make a fire,' says a little girl.

'No, that might attract the attention of the enemy.' So they all agree on a bag.

'What other hardships will little Chang encounter?'

'Hunger.'

'He's taken food with him,' says a little boy.

A little girl disagrees: 'First of all, there's nothing to eat in the village, so he can't take any food with him, and then because he'll have to walk a lot, he can't carry anything heavy.'

Everyone agrees. He may take a few sweet potatoes, but he'll have to rely on the local resources – roots and berries. So he must know how to recognize them.

'Exactly,' says the teacher. 'He knows all about them, because poor peasants were often reduced to eating wild plants when they were starving. Anyway,' she adds, 'you know some of these roots, too. Old Granny Ma brought you some the other day. But what other difficulties will Chang encounter?'

'Enemies.'

'So what will he do?'

'Think about the sufferings of his family and of his village to give himself courage. Remember that millions of peasants have already fought the enemies and liberated themselves. They seem terrifying, but really it's they who fear the poor peasants.'

'But,' another little boy adds, 'he'll have to be careful not to be noticed, and have a story ready, in case someone asks him who he is and where he's going.'

The young woman is pleased with these answers. Chang's adventures will be continued another day.

There are no fairy-tales, no stories 'just for children' and no 'wonderful world of childhood', only the right and proper inheritance that the world as it is offers children. This reminds me of a little Vietnamese child we had seen in a report about North Vietnam on television. We saw kids doing military training, learning to take the pin out of a grenade, organizing themselves to move into shelters without panic and so on. The reporter had asked 'But do you think all this military training is a suitable occupation for children?' The child replied, 'Do you think American bombs spare children? Do you think children can remain outside the war, when the whole population is being attacked? No! So it's right that the children should be prepared, and should learn to resist the aggressors.' It would be criminal not to teach them what they need to know to survive, to defend themselves, to resist.

7 Children are People

SCHOOLS UNDER CAPITALISM DON'T FREE THE FAMILY FROM ITS RESPONSIBILITY FOR CHILD-REARING

A mother's duties don't stop when her job as wet-nurse is over. All mothers know that having children doesn't only involve extra work and the time it takes — it also creates worry. Worry about their health and worry about how to bring them up. Most parents hope that their child will keep up with school work, that he or she will be a good pupil, maybe even the best in the class. The mother is willing to make great sacrifices for her child to achieve such success. She'll promise a reward if he gets good marks, she'll nag him to work, make him recite lessons fifteen times over and all because what they teach at school is competition, rivalry and individualism. Children are told; 'Go ahead! And may the best one win!' But the race is a sham. The odds are fixed long before the start. Working-class children have a different course to run from middle-class children. A tiny percentage apart, at the end of his schooling the beggar is back in the hedgerow and the working-class child is no further on than when he started. These children will be thrown on to the labour market just like their fathers, having learnt two important things at school: to mistrust one another, and that survival depends on craftiness and cunning.

Because of the dominant ethic of individualism, the working-class family (and especially the mother) can do no more than see that the child is handicapped as little as possible. The mother finds herself trapped in a contradictory situation which is a prominent feature of the feminine condition. On the one hand she owes a duty to her husband — she must look after him and take particular care that when he comes home from work he doesn't have to worry about the children and is disturbed as little as possible. In order to do that she has to instil into the children respect for their father's right to peace and relaxation. On the other hand she's a mother, expected to devote herself selflessly and exclusively to her children. It goes without saying that a woman, and especially a poor woman, is never released from these two conflicting commitments. And of the demands made on her, the more immediate imperative prevails: the mother will if necessary send her children out to play in the street, so that her husband can rest. But in so doing she becomes ever more convinced that she is personally responsible for her children's failures.

Schools under capitalism have not freed the family from their responsibility to rear their children; they have corrupted that responsibilty. It has become one which the family are not responsible *for,* in which they can't intervene because the education system has the last word anyway. It has become a 'divine curse' and nothing can be done about it.

The school is the final arbiter of worthwhile knowledge. Any experience that children, or for that matter their parents, may have gleaned outside the school is either suspect or is simply declared worthless: 'Nowadays, as a result of industrial development, working conditions have changed. Now, houses are built with cranes, coal is extracted with mechanical shovels, the worker no longer relies on brute force to accomplish his tasks. The machine does the work, and the worker controls the machine as a pilot controls his aeroplane . . .' The child of a semi-skilled worker to whom these lines are given as a dictation can only agree. He has never set foot in a factory, and if father speaks in an entirely different tone about 'industrial development', describing a world of quotas, stultifying work, authority and revolt, then father's judgement must be partial and inaccurate, since he is neither able nor entitled to challenge the veracity of the school lesson!

As long as studying is kept as a process apart from the rest of life, it will fail to affect society fundamentally. Children are taught to think that something is true because the books say it is, just as later on something will be true because the papers say it is. It is an important facet of our education system, *to discredit thoroughly and lastingly* all ideas that children or any of us might gain from lived experience, from the class struggle or from our position within society. The primary function of schools in capitalist societies is to deny that any knowledge can be found outside them. If a school lesson does happen to touch on a reality experienced by the children, that only goes to show that the reality couldn't be otherwise. The child who is used to seeing his or her mother in the role of family servant will learn at school that this is in the natural order of things and that nothing must change it. We can all remember the kind of dictations which allotted us our sex roles:

MY BIG SISTER LOVES ME

Geneviève's mother was seriously ill last month and she is still convalescing. She's too weak to take as much care of the house as she used to. Mothers do such a lot of work round the house! Nobody quite realizes it until she is no longer around, or until she is ill.

How can we get Daddy off to work as usual?

What do we have to do to make sure Geneviève gets off to school without worrying?

Luckily, big sister Monique is there. Last year she was still at school – now she stays at home. Before Daddy leaves for work, you can hear

Monique's slippers quietly shuffling on the wooden floor. The taps are running, the gas is lit: you can hear the noise of the crockery she's washing up and smell the delicious breakfast she's preparing . . .

In the afternoon, she [Monique] takes a course in shorthand-typing; and in the evening, after helping Mother and supervising Geneviève's homework, she sometimes has to stay up to do her own work.

Despite all this, she is always cheerful. When she comes home from fetching her little sister from school, it's to her that Geneviève tells her small joys and confides her little worries.

For her, Monique is a little mother.

Comprehension
1. When Mother fell ill, who took her place? What does big sister do in the house?
2. Have you got an older sister? Does she help Mother? Does she help you when Mother is too busy?
3 You may have a little brother or a little sister of your own. What do you do to help your mother with her work?

Conclusion
Big sister helps Mother and sometimes takes her place. [1]

By preventing children from using anything they might learn from daily practical experience, the education system in the West plays an important part in hindering their progress towards independence. It seeks first to cripple people and then to hand them the crutches of bourgeois values. The bourgeois school says: 'You've got bad eyesight. Here you are! Take these glasses!', and offers spectacles which only divert the people's gaze from their class experience, making them focus on an artificial world which, while resembling real life, is completely faked, signifying only the meanings imposed by the bourgeoisie. The education system chains children to their school desks and thus fundamentally directs its aim at the 'infantilization' of the future proletariat (to use an expression coined by Baudelot and Establet). [2]

As long as children remain minors, women will be oppressed. A new education system must aim to make children responsible and independent at all levels and from the earliest age. We must turn children into adults – or rather, we must radically reconstruct the distinction between 'adults' and infantile 'minors' – and thus liberate women from their roles of guardian and child-minder. Women's liberation requires a new conception of child-rearing, based on an equal relationship between adults and children which will allow the children to participate fully in all social activities. The creation of a new education system will obviously be a determining factor in transforming this relationship, and consequently a crucial one in the emancipation of women. The struggle for such a revolution in education is therefore in no way a digression from issues which affect women more closely.

CHINA – THE SCHOOL GENERATES NEW SOCIAL RELATIONS: 'LET SOCIETY BE THE CLASSROOM!'

To liberate the mother from the child is first of all to liberate the child. And that means transforming schools. Schools must be open to society and must use it like any other study material. They must create a network of multiple and reciprocal links with all manner of social activities. That is the basis of revolutionary schooling.

The students in a Nanking primary school told us about their approach to work and leisure: 'Each class regularly sets up work schedules after liaising with the neighbourhood. After discussion, we decide what jobs we'll take on. For instance our class has taken full responsibility for cleaning up several streets in the neighbourhood, and for education campaigns to teach the people about preventing illness. We appoint teams of students to carry out these tasks after school. There are also short-term plans. For example, we help the neighbourhood work team by doing the housework for a family, or we read and write letters for blind or illiterate people.'

'We practise collective mutual aid,' little Li said. *This is no empty phrase.* When I asked a little later what the difference was between individual and 'collective' friendships, little Li recounted a story that told us a lot: 'Last year my best friend fell ill. He had to stay away from school for a long time. At first I felt that he shouldn't be left all alone and that I could help him keep up with his school work if I visited him every day. But when I thought about it harder, it occured to me that my friend's illness concerned us all and that this was a good opportunity to develop "collective mutual aid". We then talked about it in class and I suggested that all the pupils should form teams who would take turns to visit him every day and help him work, take care of him, entertain him, tell him about our activities and so on. It was a good idea which helped strengthen our friendship and the unity within our ranks, and also gave greater encouragement to my friend than if I had gone to see him alone.'

'Children's palaces' further illustrate the kinds of relationships that exist between school activities and everyday life. We visited one of these children's palaces in Shanghai. It was in a splendid villa – it really was a palace in fact – built for a wealthy British capitalist a long time ago and the children had organized it into a rather special leisure centre. This house hadn't been chosen at random: we were told that the former owner had been waited on by a whole troop of servants and maids, all of whom were children. They had been treated rather worse than dogs! The worker who received us – he ran the centre – had actually been a servant in that house as a child. You can imagine what he felt now when he watched children playing ping-pong in what used to be a stately drawing-room. His job had been to work on the heating in the villa and he hadn't even been allowed into the kitchens. The building is now run by a children's committee and a workers' team, and is, like many of the children's leisure centres in China, shared by several schools. Every day schoolchildren come to it from all over the place.

The most striking thing about it was the prevailing conception of 'leisure'. We saw children playing ping-pong and others flying a remote-controlled model aeroplane they had built themselves, but we also saw children packed into a large hall and listening attentively to a party member reading a paper on the Pakistan question. Many were taking notes. Three children, sitting next to the man on the stage, were helping to lead this symposium. A group of boys and girls in the garden were practising rifle-shooting under the guidance of a PLA soldier. Watching the serious way they applied themselves to the task and the accuracy of their shooting we could see that this was no recreation. *When the nature of work and school is changed, leisure is transformed as well.* There is nothing like 'break' in our schools — because the only purpose of break time is to give children the chance to let off steam, after hours of exhausting and stupid discipline.

Games and their meaning

When you watch these children playing you understand a great deal about the new social relations. We had a long discussion with some Nanking children about their games. Anne asked them whether there were any games traditionally restricted to boys. The question puzzled them. What kind of games could possibly exclude girls? They really couldn't understand. 'Play,' they said, 'often has a useful purpose. When we go for walks in the country it gives us a chance to practise our knowledge of medicinal plants, which we gather and bring back to the neighbourhood dispensary. At other times, harvest time for example, we go for walks along the same roads as the brigades take to get to the fields, and we pick up any rice or what that has fallen off the carts and bring it back for the peasants.'

We found it hard to tell what was work and what was play in the children's descriptions of their extra-curricular activities — the words have lost their conventional meanings. When you think about it, there's something deeply disturbing about our children's play. It reflects the world we live in, while being an attempt to escape from it. Little Chinese girls and their friends don't play at: 'We'll be married, you come home tired from work and I'll have prepared some food and put the children to bed.' (Edith told me she heard her small daughter say that to her younger brother.) In China it would probably go more like this: 'There have been torrential rains breaking the dykes, and the crops are in danger of being flooded, and we've got to repair the dykes . . .', or again, as they told us, 'Practise the people's war in the countryside, learn to take a hill and hold it'.

A parallel can be drawn between children's games and art — they both reflect *and* act upon society. In capitalist society, the function of play is like the function of art for the masses: it acts as an escape, while at the same time reinforcing the dominant ideology. Children in China also have games which mirror their culture, but they don't pretend to act like 'grown-ups', and they don't try to escape from their childhood condition in their imaginations. They don't have to, because China is *their* world too, because they're not cut off from any aspect of social reality. Collective child care will not spontaneously reveal a different ideology in the children, one that was previously hidden. It must also integrate children into the society in which they live. The struggle against individualism and private interest can't possibly mean anything to children who live in a society founded on private interest and individualism. If little Jin Hua and little Tse Tang don't come to blows over a toy car, it's because they've never seen adults working their fingers to the bone to get their very own car.

The purpose of the children's palaces has always been to create new links between pupils in different schools and to enable the children to connect the school with areas outside it – especially to allow them to learn about things that aren't taught in school. Children who come to learn modelling techniques in classes given by sculptors will, in turn, teach them to their fellow-pupils. The same applies to singing, dancing, classes in instrumental music, drawing and so on. You teach others what you've learned yourself, even if you aren't fully qualified. And that's a general principle. The children's palace isn't meant to be used simply as a recreation centre, but also to allow children from different schools to meet in one place, giving them the opportunity of getting to know children other than their own school-friends. This is an important factor in broadening social interaction. The children are encouraged to be a sort of 'link' between teaching outside school and school itself. In Nanking they told us how important this had been for the children. We were given one example of a little girl who had been taught the accordion by her uncle. She then taught her comrades the techniques she'd learned. Her uncle lent her his accordion and she would take it to school so that the other children could practise on it under her direction.

Parents, children and the school
There are many more links between school and society. In the school at Nanking we were met by one of the fathers, who joined in a lengthy discussion about the role of parents in the school and outside it. 'In my opinion,' he said, 'parents play a secondary but very important role in education. They participate in the critique of the old education system. When a new school syllabus was introduced in Nanking we had frequent meetings with the teaching staff and the representatives from the workers' team at this school, to decide how we would implement the syllabus. It's important for parents to understand and be familiar with the ideological content of the childrens' education. It enables them to co-operate in their education. No doubt you know that in China each production unit and each workshop has a different day off. Now the teachers ask parents to come to the school from time to time on their rest day. We attend classes so that we can see

CHILDREN ARE PEOPLE

what the children's attitudes are in class. We also have continuing links with the teaching staff, who visit each pupil's family in turn. The parents, who know their child well, can co-operate with the teacher to help the child overcome any problems. This co-operation is crucial. The parents meet three times a term to discuss the way the school is run, any difficulties that may arise and what needs to be done. But the teachers work mainly with the pupils themselves and with the workers' team to solve problems.'

Another aspect of parent education is teaching by example. To bring up children, parents must continuously re-educate themselves, criticize their own mistakes, and accept that *children can teach them some things*. This process isn't limited to the family, it's part of a more general need to draw together words and actions, theory and practice. This reminded us of an anecdote that the instructress of a group of three-year-olds had told us when we visited a kindergarten: 'One afternoon during the little ones' rest period I took the opportunity to chat to another teacher. Several children formed a delegation to point out that I was disturbing their rest. They couldn't see why *they* had been told to keep quiet! In their opinion, they pointed out, "The rule of silence applies to everybody!".' The instructress added: 'Before that my other comrades used to tease me and would jokingly say: "Lucky you, you must have a cushy job, working with the little ones. You don't get criticized like we do!" I was very happy to be able to prove how wrong they were.'

The educational function of the family must no longer be a pretext for parental dictatorship. Socialist education is the struggle against bourgeois ideology, and the family, individually and as a whole, takes part in this struggle. A mother told us: 'I had begun to study a text of Marx, but it was very difficult and I was losing heart. I had almost decided to give up, thinking it wasn't for me, and that at my age I wasn't capable of getting down to serious study. My daughter noticed my discouragement, cheered me up, told me I ought to carry on and offered to help me. And now we study together twice a week. Thanks to my daughter's help I've been able to further my own education. It's very rewarding for me to feel that.'

POWER TO THE CHINESE CHILDREN

Allowing children *to become* educators doesn't just mean that they can criticize their parents. It involves a recognition of the political role of young people, and what could be better proof that this recognition exists than the way children actually participate in leadership? The revolutionary committees that run the primary schools are made up of teachers' representatives, members of the workers' team and schoolchildren, elected by their fellow-pupils. These schoolchildren take part in all the administrative duties of the revolutionary committee.

The nature of the relationship between teachers and pupils also reveals the importance attached to children's responsibility. It can be seen most clearly in the reform of the control of knowledge. In the first place the 'surprise attack' method has been completely abandoned and the teacher no longer tries to trap pupils. Grading, no longer a final verdict, is discussed by pupils and teachers. Pupils can often use their books and their own notes in examinations. They usually know the questions in advance. The exam is supposed to be a work of reflection and understanding, not a memory test. And above all exams have become a dual-purpose test, designed to assess both the children's knowledge and the instructor's teaching. Teachers and pupils periodically examine together the progress of one another's school work – criticizing one another during regular classroom meetings. If a teacher makes a mistake, he or she must admit it in public. If pupils are dissatisfied with a teacher's attitude and the teacher persists in his or her mistakes, they can ask the school's revolutionary committee to come and investigate the matter and take the necessary steps. A woman teacher told us; 'This procedure is a comparatively recent innovation, and we haven't had to deal with any cases yet. Classroom meetings are held every three months, but the children can of course make criticisms and suggestions to the teacher in class if necessary. And if they feel that something is seriously wrong they can ask for a general meeting to be held before the scheduled date. The workers' team attends general meetings and helps to solve problems by giving us the class position.'

Does this mean that schools are run by the pupils? It would be a serious mistake to believe that. There's no sign of infantile demagogy in Chinese educational policy. This is easy to understand. Since the children have only limited experience, they clearly haven't yet got an overall view of society. It is vitally important to extend their experience in every direction *as soon as possible*, precisely to develop their knowledge, and it is important to understand this essential point fully. '*The education of the younger generation is always in the interest of one class*', whether it's the bourgeoisie or the proletariat who educates them. However, children are said to have political responsibility, and not only are they given the right to speak out (including the right to criticize teachers and parents), but critical judgement is encouraged in itself. Mao says, 'A communist has a duty to ask himself why.' It is said, 'Children must participate in the leadership', but it is also said that 'Power lies in the hands of the working class, and it is they who educate children!' This is not as contradictory as it seems. Indeed, this question makes everything clear. It is precisely because the proletariat controls education that Chinese children have the sorts of rights and power that we never had and that our own children still haven't got. Paraphrasing Mao, we could say: 'Imperialism has its methods of schooling, we have our own, and these two opposed ways are both functions of our diametrically opposed final goals.' Giving children a voice in their affairs is just one of the ways in which the proletariat can exercise its power.

Because truth is necessarily on the side of the proletariat, it need have no fear of children constantly measuring reality against the theory they are presented with in books and on their teachers' lips. Such confrontations are even invited. Either what teachers, books and the Party say conforms

above In front of new housing in the people's commune men and women do the washing together.

below An old man takes part in the cleaning.

Thursday : weekly cleaning day in the city. Teamwork for sweeping the streets.

A young girl and boy practice shooting.

In a classroom of the University Centre of the Shanghai Machine Tool Factory men and women help each other.

Photos réalisées par l'auteur et son groupe.

A young girl heads a demonstration.

A crèche for workers from a housing complex was constructed by local inhabitants, to the right is a children's playhouse made of wood.

Boys and girls alike wash up their bowls with enthusiasm.

By the roadside leading to Chawan earthen bricks made by the members of a family dry in the sun.

Two primary school pupils in front of a machine in a production workshop.

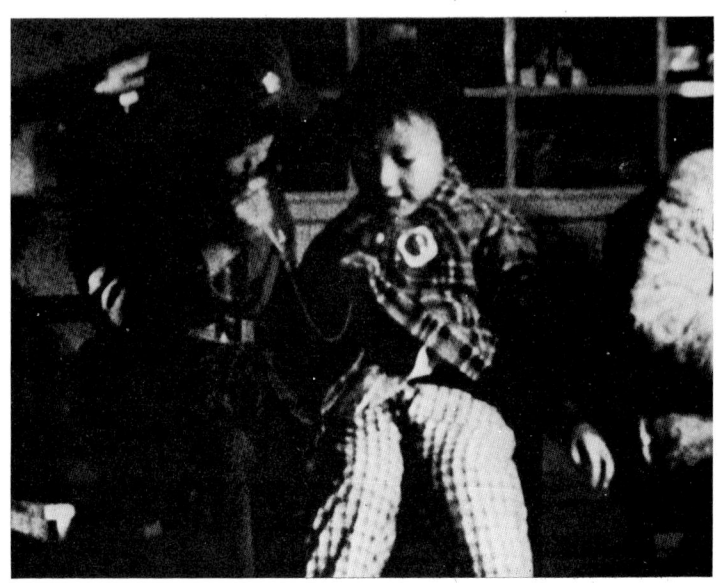

A little boy from a kindergarten practises sewing a button on the jacket of a little girl.

to reality, or reality shows that what they say is wrong. In the first case the children's experience allows them to assimilate true scientific knowledge more thoroughly and to adopt for themselves the proletarian point of view which they are taught. In the second case: 'Thank you, children, the theory you have been taught is not the proletarian point of view, and you are right to reject it'. Let's imagine for a moment that our schools were to be run according to the Chinese proletarian model. Children would go into society at large to investigate shanty towns, low-cost housing estates and private residences. They would visit factories to talk to the management, foremen and workers – even to the guards carrying revolvers in their pockets. Workers would come into the classroom to give their version of the latest large-scale strike. An immigrant worker would come to talk about his experiences and his ideas about colonialism. The children would be organized, and they would be free to speak out. At the end of a lesson, they might well criticize the teacher. What would be left of absolute respect for teachers, of discipline? What would be left of the capitalist school? let society be the classroom! But not every class can allow this to happen. Marx has shown that bourgeois ideology is an inverted, mystified reflection of reality, whereas the ideology of the proletariat is scientific and hence really provable. If it's true that the bourgeoisie inculcates its ideology in to our schools (as the proletariat does in its own schools), then we can see why the apparent contradiction we met above was purely subjective and not an objective reality.

One aspect of children's independence

This new kind of upbringing and education inevitably results in a severing of the rigid ties by means of which parents and teachers (albeit in different ways) keep children in a state of dependence. The exercise of paternal authority is facilitated in capitalist countries by the family's responsibility in providing materially for the growth and upbringing of the younger generation. This responsibility is sufficiently far-reaching to support the father's authority in all but the comparatively rare cases where the law is called in. All the talk about children's liberation is meaningless until we realize that that material reliance on even one person is the very denial of the possibility of independence. A child who is totally deprived of autonomy can choose only between parents and the street, with all the risks that entails. This situation is not usually criticized because it seems perfectly natural: how could children support themselves? The solution isn't to transform children into wage earners. *In China, too, parents assume material responsibility for their children, but in China the responsibility is not theirs exclusively.* That's the crucial difference.

Youth centres, like the Shanghai children's palace described earlier, are free for of charge. Sporting events, film shows and theatrical performances are all free schoolchildren: either children (all children, it isn't a form of reward) are allowed in without paying, or else schools regularly hand out tickets. Whenever children stay in peoples' communes they become the responsibility of the brigade. The socialization of housework means that they don't have to depend, everywhere and at all times, on their mothers for their everyday needs. In short, while parents continue to support their children, society as a whole also takes a large share of the responsibility. Children who never have to limit their studies or their cultural, leisure and sporting activities because of their parents' limited financial resources can be truly independent.

THE TRANSMISSION OF KNOWLEDGE IS THE TRANSMISSION OF A CLASS POSITION

Chinese people say that before the Cultural Revolution their schools were organized on the Russian model, which in turn duplicated the capitalist school. They had marks, punishments, awards, reprimands, teachers' authority – the panoply of props for a classic educational farce. But because the people had already begun to overthrow social relations in some spheres; because the proletariat had overthrown the power of the old exploiting classes; because new moral values based on collectivism had seen the light of day, the educational system was in clear contradiction to the revolution. And wherever the revolutionary forces were firmly in control there was great opposition to the schools – sometimes so much so that workers and peasants would themselves create new schools, to be controlled by the masses.

The first stage of the critique of the old educational system was to reveal its class character. The local and national newspapers of the time are full of articles refuting the classical bourgeois thesis according to which education is simply a neutral technique for communicating neutral knowledge. These articles argue Mao's position that: 'Education is always a response to a class's need for self-perpetuation. The proletariat seeks to transform the world according to its own world outlook, and so does the bourgeoisie. In this respect, the question of which will win out, socialism or capitalism, is still not really settled.' And so the notion gained currency that educational methods are not simply means of varying efficiency for transmitting universally true knowledge to children, but are, in reality, the political and ideological tools of one class, which has decreed that ideas serving its interests are true for the whole of society. Mao says: '*In schools, all activities aim to transform the students' ideology.*' The ideas propagated by slave-owners justified slavery; bourgeois ideas justify capitalism; the ideas communicated by the proletariat are designed to fashion the younger generations' ideology in line with revolutionary values. This destroys at the root the possibility of the proletariat using the methods used in bourgeois schools. Replacing the academic study of bourgeois history textbooks by the academic study of a few Marxist books, even if they are Mao Tse-tung's works, will never enable the proletariat to train those who are to take up the revolutionary cause.

If the proletariat is to educate the younger generation, it must at the very least be allowed to play an active part in education, playing *its own* part in the political and ideological leadership and acquiring the necessary experience in the field. Until now the members of the proletariat used to go to school only as pupils, never as teachers. Of course working-class children have sometimes become teachers in capitalist countries. But then they ceased to be long to the proletariat. And as the educational system was still controlled by the bourgeoisie, they would become mere cogs in its machinery. It has never been a question of 'proletarianizing' the recruitment of teachers, though this is still a necessary step to take, but rather of ensuring that the working class, which is involved in today's revolutionary struggle, should overthrow the educational system as it now exists, and assume control of education. So it was that in China, during the summer of 1968, groups of workers, elected by their workmates, went into schools to seize power in primary and secondary education. [3]

In the Nanking primary school a woman teacher told us about the visit one of these teams paid to her school: 'It was in the autumn of 1968. Several neighbourhood factories chose a few workers to help to revolutionize teaching. Teachers are at the heart of the contradiction. They have the power in schools, they are absolute rulers, but who are they? The majority have a working-class background, but this certainly does not necessarily make them experts in a new form of education. "What links had we kept with the masses?" – that was an awkward question.

'In fact we were cut off from the concerns of the people. Our only object was to make sure that pupils kept up with the curriculum and passed their examinations, but we didn't ask ourselves whether what we taught was useful to the revolution. This atmosphere encouraged children to become bookworms. They were learning so as to get good marks, to pass exams and to move up next year. They were becoming indifferent to politics, to society and to the rest of the world.'

At this point a little boy interrupted the teacher to back her up: 'Before the Cultural Revolution, whenever my mother asked my brother to prepare the meal, or to look after us, because she had to go out to work with other comrades, my brother would answer, 'It's not my job to do that, I've got to get on with my school work. I've got homework to do and if I don't do it I'll get bad marks." My mother would always get angry, "What kind of school is it where children learn to be selfish and to succeed without any concern for the collective good?" '

'Little Li's story,' resumed the teacher, 'shows that we hadn't taken the needs of the masses as a starting-point. Under the pretext of transmitting pure intellectual knowledge, we were in fact imparting a reactionary ideology. How could we presume to form the new generation of revolutionaries while we kept them out of touch with the revolution?'

When Chinese teachers tell us that what was wrong with the old system was that it didn't serve the people, they mean that the educational system wasn't furthering the people's fundamental interest in arming the younger generation with the means of making a materialist critique by linking theory and practice, thus enabling the young to carry the revolution *consciously* into all areas of life.

New teaching methods and their class nature
In that school in Nanking we probably saw the clearest and most concrete examples of the links being forged between theory and practice, teaching and manual work, school and society, pupils, teachers and the masses. There, as in all other schools, boys and girls between the ages of seven and twelve undergo an important experience. The leader of the revolutionary committee explained that to begin with the new teaching system created since the Cultural Revolution was still at an experimental stage, and that the process of struggle-criticism-reform was still developing. For instance at the end of 1971 there was still no national school syllabus for primary schools.

During the Cultural Revolution the various revolutionary committees of the schools in Nanking drew up a temporary syllabus and wrote their own textbooks based on criticisms of the old educational system formulated by a vast movement of pupils, teachers, parents and workers' teams. The Committee leader told us that it hadn't been decided whether or not to reinstate a national school syllabus using the same textbooks in all schools. That could be dealt with later. The important things now were for large numbers of people, including teachers themselves in the first place, to collaborate to draw up new curricula following the political guidelines laid down during the Cultural Revolution and ensuring that all school-leavers were brought up to the same national educational level.

The curriculum is now divided into five subject areas: politics, literature, arithmetic, physical education and art (drawing and singing). In the two senior classes two new subjects are added: foreign languages (usually English or Russian) and natural science. There is a class specifically devoted to politics, but all the other subjects are politically based. The Chinese lesson, for example, is at the same time a lesson on the history of the revolution, and when the children study grammar, they do so in texts about the Paris Commune or the war against the Japanese.

The country's newspapers have an important part to play too, and are used as school text books. The same approach is evident in arithmetic teaching. Children learn to invent their own problems, starting from the real questions that have to be faced in daily life. Absurd and unreal questions of the 'tap-filling-a-leaking-bath' variety would be greeted by the children with: 'Why let the bath leak instead of repairing it?' And when children calculate how much time is needed to irrigate a field of area X, from a source supplying volume Y of water per minute to Z irrigation canals, they also calculate that this time could be reduced by half if blade-wheels were to be set up at the mouth of the canals to increase the water flow.

I asked one of the children whether they ever disagreed with the policies of the government and what would happen if so. They laughed when my question was translated to them. 'Of course we disagree sometimes. Would you like an example?' The boy who answered was a ten-year-old. 'Well, not long ago there were disagreements about Nixon's visit. I, for example, felt it was unacceptable that the leading representative of United States imperialism should be allowed to visit our socialist country. Our form mistress suggested that we should carry out some inquiries among children in other classes, our families and other workers to find out what the general opinion was. She also suggested that we should study the global situation more throughly to place the question in context. So we spent a lot of our free time debating the question in our families and during public meetings in the neighbourhood. It took some time and some serious study to come to an understanding. Now I agree that Nixon should come.'

'Can you tell us how you justify that?' we asked him.

'Yes. You must understand one thing. It wasn't us who rejected relations with the United States. We have always been prepared to establish relations with all countries on the proper basis. But the United States government, hoping that our revolution would be defeated, set up an economic and political blockade against China. The United States took over Taiwan, a Chinese province, for military reasons, installed Chiang Kai-shek and proclaimed him 'the authentic representative of China'. They gave Taiwan a seat at the United Nations and denied China's existence. Well, now Nixon is coming in person to visit a country that has been crossed off his own world map. That's a victory for a start! And it's mainly due to the defeats that the people of Asia have inflicted on the United States, forcing it to revise some of its attitudes towards us. We are well aware that you have to rely on the people of a country to overthrow its reactionary policies. Establishing relations with the United States will encourage mutual exchange and understanding between our peoples.

'The reactionaries of the world slander China, and want people to believe that she would make war on other countries to impose her own political system on them. Refusing to invite Nixon would deprive us of a means of denying these slanders. Undoubtedly some people will also seize on Nixon's visit here to claim that our government is capable of modifying its attitude towards other peoples' struggles or its support of them. But China's support of world revolutionary struggles has not been due to the refusal of some states to recognize the Chinese government. This support exists because our government is a dictatorship of the proletariat, which places great emphasis on the international proletariat. The fact that some governments are now beginning to re-establish relations with us doesn't change our position in any way. The best way to prove this beyond doubt is to agree to Nixon's visit, since he himself has asked to come. Nations will judge our attitude on the evidence, and this will be the best testimony. And that's why I'm happy for Nixon to come.'

Jenny asked the teacher to explain the principles guiding her in giving lessons in politics. 'We do our best to present all sides of the problem, so that the children can bring more knowledge to bear on the question. We must arm the children, and ourselves, with the tools of analysis and materialist critique. We make sure of allowing those who hold opposite opinions, or those who are hesitant, to express their doubts and criticisms, even if they are in a very small minority and even if their criticisms are totally wrong. This enables the pupils to criticize mistaken points of view and it's instructive for everyone. We must learn to think. We don't want to instil in the younger generation the docile submissiveness that Liu Shao-chi preached. The revolution needs enthusiastic and profound adherence, not just formal consent. *The class struggle is all around us. The important thing is to teach children to fight consciously.*'

History as told by its makers

We attended a lesson on the history of the class struggle. The grandfather of one of the pupils came to tell a class of twenty-five children the story of his childhood and adolescence in the China of yesterday. The old man had begun to tell his story a few minutes before we were taken to sit at the back of the classroom, and even though our visit had aroused quite a bit of curiosity in the school, not one of the pupils budged when we entered. Not a single one of them turned round to glance at us, even furtively. They were completely absorbed by the old man's tale, hanging on his every word and reliving his every experience.

Could such a thing happen in the West? Could an ordinary working man, with little education, come to school in his overalls and tell his story, with the whole class listening in silence, enthralled? He was thin and seemed to have suffered dreadfully; his hands were gnarled, the hands of an old manual worker. He spoke with few gestures and no melodrama. He stood there without embarrassment, but also without the facile pomposity of the professional lecturer. Sometimes he would recall the poverty in which his family and all the people had been kept by the local landowners. At such moments his voice betrayed his anger. And as I listened I thought that people can never stop rebelling against the oppression they have had to suffer, even long after it has ceased. This is, without doubt, a precious legacy handed down by the generation which has borne the worst ills of exploitation and which has risen and destroyed the old order. It is a great revolutionary heritage for the younger generation.

The importance that transmitting the lessons of the past has for the future can be gauged by the relentless way in which the bourgeoisie has tried, and is still trying, to prevent our people from taking possession of the history of revolutionary struggles – the Paris Commune, for example. What they're doing is *defrauding* us of our inheritance. Oppressed masses easily identify with these revolutionary struggles of the past, even those that developed long ago and arose out of apparently quite different conditions.

These 'evocations of the past', which play such an important part in China's daily cultural life, are of great significance. They are her history, as told by the people and created by them. They represent a recognition, through the facts, that it is up to the people to judge what is good and what is bad. Furthermore, it is the right of those who have made history themselves to relate it to the young. And that is a most significant way in which the history of the revolution and, essentially, the seizure of power by the poor under the leadership of the working class, becomes a 'national culture' with which the younger generations can identify and which they can turn into a contemporary morality.

The pupils at Nanking put on a show for us. One of the acts was a playlet staged by the children themselves. It was based on the account an old peasant woman had given them of her past life. In one of the scenes the mother – the peasant woman as played by a little girl of about ten – watched her child being dragged away from her by the landowner's bailiffs because she hadn't been able to pay her taxes. The mother fought the bailiffs tooth and nail to get her child back. They threw her brutally on to the ground and she let out a heart-rending scream. At first she wept, but then we saw her switch from despair to hatred. A sense of indignation gradually swept over her and she rose to her feet, dry-eyed, resolute, fierce and indomitable. It was overwhelming, and very much more accessible for us than the opera we saw in Peking. It seemed to us that even if this evocation of the past was used merely to create a cultural tradition, the children related to it with such conviction and warmth that that would make it valuable in itself. What a splendid way to take their revenge for the culture the bourgeoisie imposed on the people, in which they were represented as ignorant, brutish and sheep-like stooges.

GIRLS SHOOTING AND BOYS SEWING: REAL CO-EDUCATION

Co-education doesn't just mean putting boys and girls together. It must also mean teaching them exactly the same things. And domestic science is one of the most important areas in which to test the reality or otherwise of co-education.

In the Soviet Union the widespread return to the woman-at-home ideology after 1936 soon affected children's upbringing and education. This ideological switch was directly connected to the Soviet regime's need to return to the family its economic function, wherever that had been even marginally destroyed. It straightforwardly accepted that all the economic and ideological functions of the bourgeois family were needed to develop 'society'. The extremely reactionary nature of this return to the earlier family structure is nakedly revealed in the reasons given by the Soviet leadership to justify separate education for boys and girls:

> We have taken steps to enable schools to adapt in every respect to the special characteristics of boys and girls. The Soviet State today is faced with important problems, the first of which is how to strengthen the primary unit of society – the family – on the premise that the father and the mother are completely equal as heads of the family *but that each has*

his or her own very clearly defined tasks. Therefore, we must institute a scholarly regime which educates young men to become the fathers of the future, brave warriors for their motherland, and young women to become conscientious mothers, the educators of the next generation. [4]
And so boys are called upon to become soldiers, girls to rear future soldiers!

Orlov justified the measure introducing the progressive winding-up of co-education in the 20 August 1943 issue of *Izvestia* in the following terms: 'In co-education neither the peculiarities of the physical development of boys and girls, nor the *different* requirements of their *vocational training* ... can receive proper attention ... It is essential to introduce in girls' schools such additional subjects as pedagogics, needlework, courses in domestic science.' [5] Similarly in April 1945 Timofeev stated in the official Soviet education journal: 'Socialist humanitarianism must take account of the *feminine nature*. We must maintain women's interest in beautiful objects, flowers, elegant clothes and ornaments.' [6]

Domestic-science classes – the sound of the words was enough to make our hearts sink. Jeanne was reminded of those Wednesday afternoons when the boys left the classroom and the girls took out a little square of white fabric on which they practised overcasting seams, hemming, open-work or herringbone stitch, waiting for the big day when they would be able to make a child's vest. The immeasurable boredom of those endless afternoons when our coloured thread outlined the grey and monotonous future that awaited us. We could hear the shouts of the boys playing football under our windows, adding insult to injury. They could play games, they were outside in the fresh air, lucky them! But Jeanne was really wrong to despise domestic science. It played a most important part in fermenting our feminine revolt.

In Peking's secondary school no. 26 domestic science classes are very different. Boys and girls perform a variety of services side by side. A shoe-mender's workshop had been set up in a little room and when we visited it children were sitting on stools mending slippers and resoling canvas shoes. They greeted us in silence, although a few moments earlier we'd heard their chattering from the corridor outside. We saw several other workshops for repairing the pupils' clothes. In one a boy of thirteen or fourteen was skilfully sewing a large patch on a trouser seat. [7] In another room children were cutting their friends' hair. Another room was a proper carpentry workshop. Boys and girls went there to repair school equipment, to learn how to make benches and, more generally, to do the sort of odd jobs that crop up every day. Yet another room housed a clinic where the children were using acupuncture to treat one another's minor ailments and learning to recognize medicinal plants and to prepare herbal remedies. The pupils took turns doing these various services, helped by workers or teachers.

Domestic science is not only truly co-educational, it also has immediate practical value. Just think how much a mother can be 'liberated' if her children look after their own clothes and shoes and take care of their health at school, in other words if they're self-reliant. Once again, that's the extraordinary thing about the Chinese revolution. The mother's work has not been taken over by 'state services', *on which the children would be just as dependent*. Work which was once the province of the family alone (i.e. of women) has become a collective responsibility, shared by all sectors of society.

But before this result can be achieved a whole world of prejudice has to be overturned the whole gamut of beliefs justifying the division of labour on grounds of natural inequality has to be combated. Old ideas must be uprooted – ideas which attribute innate qualities of initiative and authority to men, and which allow women greater 'sensitivity' only because this makes it easier to deny them any aptitude for intellectual work. Children must be shown that no one is born more suited to intellectual work than manual work, more gifted at housework than at foreign languages. It's a perpetual ideological struggle, and one whose effectiveness in China is based on a system of education that places no restrictions on the spheres of learning and activity that girls may enter. Apprenticeship for the people's war involves children – and girls aren't kept out of it. Like the boys, they are given military training, practise rifle-shooting, run assault courses and learn the rudiments of unarmed combat. In every school and in all activities outside school, children receive military training, handle weapons, organize themselves into platoons and learn to protect themselves and to dig shelters.

LINKING STUDIES TO PRODUCTIVE WORK

All pupils undergo some training in productive work for about a week in every school year, in the workshops built inside the schools by local residents. This has nothing to do with the services *I* mentioned above. Those workshops have an entirely different purpose.

No attempt is made to give children on abstract or old-fashioned conception of manual work, unlike in France where 'manual work' always refers to craftsmanship – the blacksmith, the mason and the carpenter are still the basic material for dictation and memorized prose passages in primary schools, even though such occupations have almost entirely disappeared. In France the kind of work most people have to do in a modern industrial society is rarely, if ever, mentioned. Assembly lines and quotas are ignored – and for good reason. In the few contexts in which they are mentioned, the idea is to paint an abstract picture which is far from innocent.

The popular image of the manual worker is the eighteenth-century journeyman, who has mastered his craft, loves his work and relishes the knowledge that his is a difficult job well done – difficulty no longer implies laboriousness but merely the skilful application of craft.

The small workshops in schools

At the school at Nanking we were told that the workshops had been set up after very close links had been established with a neighbouring lorry-manufacturing plant. The factory workers had come to install some of their machines and had organised a simple labour process but one that would enable the children to carry out some of the operations performed in the factory. The children were making air-filters for the factory.

A woman worker from the factory, a member of the workers' team, worked in these little workshops. She took the children through all the necessary steps and taught them simple techniques, thus enabling them to acquire manual skill very quickly. But in particular she made them realize the importance of *collective work*, of being united, for the creation of wealth. These small school workshops ('our' workshops they call them) are the sole responsibility of the children, who organize and run them more or less alone, and give them a chance to acquire experience that is different from what they would get by actually going into a factory.

Although the workshops have actual machines from the factory, they involve a relatively small number of operations; the work process is very simple, so that the children are better able to master the work and to grasp its overall meaning. They are therefore also better able to introduce innovations, to invent new procedures and to judge what is good and what needs changing. One of the most important things is to ensure that the child's first contact with productive work isn't a training in blind discipline, but is instead closely linked to the collective exercise of *power*.

If you look at it more closely it becomes clear that all this is a necessary counterbalance to the rest of school teaching. Even if class work is done collectively and the children help one another instead of jealously guarding their own knowledge, individual learning of reading, writing and arithmetic still prevails. Hence the experience of production, which can *only* function collectively, is vital if they are to adopt socialist attitudes. The children are getting ready to become, as Marx might have put it, freely associated collective workers.

They would come to the workshops during schoolhours and follow the same rhythm as the other pupils – three forty-five-minute sessions in the morning and two in the afternoon, each one separated by a ten-minute break. The younger children would work in the workshops only in the morning. Jeanine asked the children whether they thought of the workshops as a game. They were deeply shocked by the question: 'Not at all,' replied one of them. 'The question of the workshops is a very important one. How could we ever continue what the workers and peasants have started if our studies were remote from practical work, if we had no concrete knowledge of production and no links with the workers and the peasants? We couldn't!"

Productivity isn't the most important part of this work. Making children work isn't an attempt to capitalize on every available source of labour in society, children included. *The work is instructive for the children because* it's useful to society; and it's useful to society mainly because it's instructive for the children.

Alongside the workshops are vegetable gardens, which are cultivated by the children all the year round on a team rota system. They provide a high proportion of the vegetables eaten in the canteen. There are vegetable gardens everywhere, even in the heart of the city. Sometimes they even had to dig up the pavements and streets to find the countryside under the cobblestones.

Productive work outside school

These aren't the only links the children have with social production, however.

The school year proper lasts eight and a half months. When the year is over pupils and teacher spend three weeks in a peoples' commune, to take part in the farm work. They live with peasant families and learn about the conditions of life and work in the country. This gives them an opportunity to swop experiences and broaden their horizons. The peasants, we were told, welcome them warmly and take a great deal of trouble to give them a class education. They have cultural evenings when the city children perform plays for the peasants and vice versa. They are given concrete evidence about the struggles of the past and told about those of the present. The children gain an understanding, 'supported by proof', of the creativity of the peasant masses and of the progress they have led the whole Chinese people to make.

Chinese children are not irresistibly drawn to the cities and after leaving school they are as likely to settle in rural areas as anywhere else. It is fundamental party policy (though those who have a bourgeois conception of industrialization oppose it) not to urbanize China, but to develop industry in the countryside itself using the existing agricultural brigades. Of course carrying out this policy is possible only in so far as the 'country bumpkin' is not an object of contempt socially, and it depends on a clear understanding, especially among children from an early age, of the importance of the peasantry to the revolution and of the need to narrow the gap between town and country.

After their stay in the country, the children often work in a factory for two or three weeks. Obviously, as in the country, they don't do all the jobs an adult does, and their working day isn't as long. But they are there in the workshops, among the workers, and they work beside them. Here again, the acquisition of technical knowledge cannot be separated from the ideological and political training they receive. They take part in the workers' own cultural and political activities. This gives some idea of the esteem in which these children are held. They become, so we are told, apprentices under worker-masters.

Study is emphasized in this work, too. It is not at all a matter of teaching them the tricks of the trade that enable them to perform certain operations without understanding their significance. The purpose of the techniques used is explained to them in detail – why this part must be screwed and that one soldered; how the work done here is only a part of the whole work process, deriving its value and meaning from the collective involvement of others, before and after, in communal production.

The children also have concrete experience of the shortcomings in work processes today. Great care is taken to make them share the interest with which workers approach technological development and to show them how they achieve it through close collaboration with the technicians. The struggle between the two attitudes that pervades the whole question of technological progress is constantly stressed. The children must not suffer from the illusion that the development of productive forces is neutral and politically inconsequential.

8 Child-rearing and Education: the Province of Society or of the State

Child-rearing and education raise a number of other points. Clearly, child-rearing in China is no longer the exclusive province of the individual family, but equally clearly, it is not the province of specialists. The Soviet Union's experience in this area also offers a contrast that helps us to grasp the full significance of the Chinese experience.

'There is no doubt that the terms "my parents", "our children" will gradually fall out of usage, being replaced by such conceptions as "old people", "adults", "children" and "infants". Lunacharsky's comments [1] were intended to support the thesis that children would have to stop being the property of parents and become the property of the State. The question of children is, at bottom, the question of society's future. Do we want to retain our division of labour and the present structure of social roles, or do we want to destroy them? If the latter, how can we hope to do it if child-rearing is entirely in the hands of a body of State specialists? That kind of upbringing and education is the best way to cut children off from the real body of society and to fix for ever in their psyche the attitude of the eternal minor, constantly subjected to the tutelage of specialists who always and in all circumstances 'know better' and are 'more competent'. The property relationships between parents and their submissive children must disappear. But there is a wider-ranging underlying social relationship which so to speak, delegates, the guardianship of children to their parents. This doesn't strike only against children, but against all oppressed people. It assigns to children the role of 'minors', deprived of autonomy and of responsibility. This relationship is created by cutting children off from society and keeping them in a world apart, the 'childhood world' of school and family. Lunacharsky's new perspective merely reinforced this relationship.

Although it doesn't seem like it, the question of children is basically that of the State. Socialism, which is the transitional period between capitalism and communism, is precisely the destruction of the old State and the building of a new one, albeit a rather peculiar new State, since its goal is its own eventual disappearance – the State to end all States. It's no surprise, then, that this question is the stumbling block of all possible revisionist falsifications, because in this area more than in any other the bourgeoisie, which formerly had a total monopoly within the State, remains strong for a very long time after being overthrown. Even though the bourgeoisie also controlled the factories, it obviously could not stop the workers running them, and therefore knowing them thoroughly.

The Chinese system of child-rearing and education is a striking example of the new type of State whose strength lies in its own ultimate destruction. The proletariat increases its power by means of the direct and effective exercise of leadership over more and more sectors of society, thus destroying the monopoly of the traditional leadership. Because the proletariat has strengthened itself and because its ideology is strong enough to dominate in certain areas, the masses are beginning to control child-rearing, even taking some parts of it into their own hands. As a result there is no longer a monopoly of State specialists in this field – notably in the education system, but also in the ancillary medical or mental health services and so on. This is the significance of the entry of the working class into hospitals and offices as well as into schools and universities, in the form of workers' propaganda teams responding to Mao Tse-tung's appeal: 'The working class – and not *just* its *party* or its *army* – must exercise leadership in everything.'

But we should not jump to the conclusion that the Chinese workers' State is disintegrating. Indeed it could be said that it has never been stronger. But its strength is different from the strength of all repressive States because it is derived from mass power and the continuously reinforced capacity for social leadership that the working class and its allies now exercise. The Cultural Revolution demonstrated to a striking degree that an increase in mass power is always the result of a ruthless struggle between the proletariat and the bourgeoisie. And the more this power grows, *the more the State machinery loses its monopoly of leadership*. And the more the State machinery loses its monopoly, the stronger the State becomes as the instrument and expression of the power of the workers and of the masses.

'Political' experts no longer have a monopoly, of leadership. As the masses' ability to lead increases, so the need for leadership decreases; the machinery of leadership is cut back and simplified at all levels and the different forms of organization of the masses take over an increasing number of functions.

THE MYTH OF SELF-EDUCATION

Today we are beginning to understand how bourgeois ideas of education succeed in transforming the majority of children into the submissive beings we know. But we should also be aware of the other means which the bourgeoisie has of preventing children from acquiring the proletarian point of view.

Broadly speaking, there are two ways of maintaining the inferior status of the proletariat. They can either be forbidden access to the academic 'reserves' of science, technology, philosophy and art, being told that they are not really bright enough; or, conversely, they can be told that their intelligence is intuitive and innate, that they can draw all necessary knowledge from their *current* experience, and that therefore it's not worth their while to poke their noses into scientific or philosophical matters. These recommendations are accompanied by calls to destroy schools, universities and institutes. All this is done with the aim of preventing the proletariat from acquiring any experience through the reform of these areas and the transformation of the intelligentsia, who will have been the sole officiators.

The revisionists in China, the spokesmen of the bourgeoisie, have held these two attitudes one after the other. They held the first before the Cultural Revolution, switching to the second while it was taking place as a diversionary ploy. This was an attempt to remain in power while concealing their policy of capitalist restoration under the guise of an ultra-left line.

Similarly, bourgeois society has two ways of preventing children from shaking off their infant status.

The first has already proved itself historically in the authoritarian and 'scholastic' capitalist education system, with its ideology of talent, its separate educational streams and, most of all, the absolute dichotomy between school 'work' and production and between the model purity of scientific research and the reality of the class struggle. So familiar are the products of this system, that further details are unnecessary.

But bourgeois society has yet another technique up its sleeve, and a much more devious one – devious because to all intents and purposes it is diametrically opposed to the established system, yet its practical results are identical. It is represented by the policy of *free and undirected self-education* of children. But here, too, the old bourgeois theory of human nature is at work. The idea is that children's repression is like a spring being compressed: remove the force that holds them back and they will bounce back into their natural shape.

What could be more left-wing in appearance than aiming to free children from all restraints and even from any outside interference? As its name suggests, self-education dispenses with instructors, allowing the children to be their own teachers. But just as unsupported bodies in free fall are attracted by the earth's gravitational pull, so the unhindered child in a 'free' school will be attracted by the dominant force of bourgeois ideology – and perhaps with even more insidious results. Indeed nothing works better at concealing the backstage educators, society's rulers, than a theory which claims that there are no educators. Society is still there, and there are always educators. It's better that they should give their names and show their faces.

In the Soviet Union in the twenties many and varied educational experiments were made. These efforts and the ideas behind them, although displaying several genuinely left-wing aspects, often carried with them a certain number of mistaken attitudes. The ideological lines that were then being drawn didn't come out of thin air. They were born of the experience that progressive educational groups had gained while fighting Tsarism. But these positions didn't constitute a definitive proletarian point of view on schools and education. The masses hadn't yet had a chance to ponder these questions within their own experience, or to verify the correctness of certain ideas, or to develop new ideas and criticize mistaken attitudes. Many idealistic viewpoints, and especially those held by bourgeois democrats, had been taken simply and uncritically from educational trends in the West (from Dewey, for example). The struggle against quasi-feudal and ultra-repressive tsarist education reinforced the idea, which is especially noticeable in the work of Blonsky and Lepechinsky, that a child's nature had to be freed from outside influence and allowed full expression. Clearly, the best way to do this is to ensure that nothing in children's 'environment' can control their education, because that would misshape, repress and suppress their rich nature.

Shatsky, a typical example of a non-Bolshevik progressive educationalist, gives a very clear illustration of this sort of deviation. He was a firm proponent of the theory of education for its own sake and experimented with children's communes run by those who lived there, applying the principle of complete autonomy for children. The experience of these communes should have revealed the erroneous character of idealist presuppositions about children's 'nature'. They were a complete failure.

For one thing, none of these children's communes managed to dispense with teachers altogether, and children's education was directed, not by the proletariat and society as a whole, but by specialists acting on their behalf. Moreover, even though they had been isolated in order to protect them from 'evil influences' and to offer them the 'protection' that was thought necessary to the generation of egalitarian communist principles, it soon became clear that these societies of children were reproducing the prevalent features of class society. Typically bourgeois forms of ideology appeared, and the children, since they were more radically cut off from the ongoing struggles against the bourgeoisie than usual, were even less able to fight them. Krupskaya was eventually led to oppose the right of these children to hold courts of justice and inflict punishments. 'Because,' she said, 'these courts purely and simply reproduce adult courts of law, even if no adults take part in them.'

We know how children's gangs will spontaneously reproduce relationships of bourgeois discipline and oppression. Little boys and little girls who go to the same school and who have never been explicitly told about the inferiority of women will quite and quickly reproduce among themselves the pattern of male superiority, so that, for example, girls are excluded from the noble games of war and marbles. Furthermore, the friendships between boys and girls will precisely imitate the ultra-conventional models of society. Little boys, like men, have straightforward friendships, playfully aggressive, faithful but not mawkish, like those their fathers formed during the war. Little girls' friendships are petty, full of jealousy and possessiveness, friendships for ever and ever – until the first peccadillo turns them into savage hatreds. Just like mummy's friends! The wonderful world of childhood? What utter nonsense! The reality is a world in which all our society's laws, contradictions, struggles and moral values can be found. Children may be kept apart from society, but they are still hampered by their inevitable dependence on adults and know only their obligations to society. They know nothing of the few rights they have, or of the means they have to fight against that society. Of course there can be no handier situation for making sure that any prejudice necessary to society will be accepted as divine and eternal law, and for inspiring docile submissiveness and blind obedience.

Once again, everything seems to be for the best in the best of all capitalist worlds. Schools and families seem to share happily the task of turning the child into the sort of citizen capitalism needs. But this is only on the surface. Between the educational machinery and the family there is not only a division of the labour of repression, there are also violent contradictions; and particularly, of course, contradictions between the school and the working-class family. Not to see this is tantamount to depriving the revolution of one of its key levers in the class struggle. The equation of the question of children with the question of the future is just as valid for us as it is for a socialist country. A revolutionary movement that does not recognize the importance of children's liberation is a suicidal movement, and, in the last analysis not a revolutionary movement at all.

RECOGNIZING THE TWO SIDES OF MOTHERHOOD: RE-PRESSED AND REPRESSIVE

To see in children only the work that they create and the resulting slavery that women endure is a profoundly reactionary view in two senses. Firstly, it ignores the fact that the revolution's ultimate goal is the emancipation of all humanity, including children. Secondly, it carefully hides the fact that while children are a source of work, anxiety and anguish for their families, and mainly for their mothers, they are *above all* the victims of often unintentional maternal repression. Nevertheless it is still true that 'We've had enough of kids and work and washing' is a deeply reactionary slogan which puts oppressed children, capitalist exploitation and domestic oppression in the same category. It confuses what one must struggle against with those who one must struggle with and for. It's the slogan of the nihilist petty-bourgeois, who, although oppressed, is incapable of conceiving of a revolutionary project which would radically alter his or her condition.

It is inconceivable that a revolutionary women's movement could ignore the question of children, just as it is inconceivable that a proletariat which ignores the other sectors of society could hope to take any revolutionary movement to a successful conclusion. We have no right to demand equality between people if we don't *immediately* take up again the question of the relations of oppression that bind us to children.

There are many people who, while conscious of the importance of children, fail to make the proper analysis of the causes of children's oppression. The women's movement is mistaken when it sees this oppression as solely the consequence of the existence of family units producing selfishness and private interest. Of course the bourgeois family (i.e. a unit which functions in bourgeois society, and not necessarily a unit whose members are from the bourgeoisie) produces such an ideology. But that's not because of its nuclear structure, nor because of the official monogamy among parents, nor because children live with their parents – all of which are Women's Liberation Movement arguments. If the family 'runs on selfishness' it's because selfishness is an inherent and necessary feature of capitalism. The Cultural Revolution clearly exposed this fact, as can be seen in the slogan of the time: 'Fight self and criticize revisionism.' Selfishness is nothing less than bourgeois ideology. And bourgeois ideology is created by capitalism; it is a result of the way in which the capitalist system produces all the material conditions of life, including the family structure itself. The self-centredness engendered by the family is an effect and not a cause of capitalist and other exploiting societies. As long as the wage system exists, as long as that relation between labour power expended and the 'damages' paid in the form of wages survives, there will be a material basis for selfishness to exist and develop. And this basis remains throughout the period of transition from capitalism to communism, even though it is enfeebled and withering away (see p. 000).

It is thoroughly idealistic to imagine that forming a commune where several couples and their children live together will affect this situation to any appreciable extent. At best, familial selfishness will be replaced by communal selfishness. Anyone in need of convincing has only to observe how quickly communes turn in on themselves and devote themselves to their own internal problems, isolating themselves from society and in so doing repeating the pattern they criticize in the conventional family. To the extent that the adult members of a commune fail to live in complete autarchy and still have contacts with society, they are inevitably bearers of the dominant ideology. And even if the children were cut off from society apart from these adults – an absurd situation if they are claiming to struggle against sectarian clannishness – that contact alone would be enough to reproduce in those children the most marked features of the society their parents have fled from. The situation is exactly the same as when those exceedingly possessive mothers, steeped in the rights of motherhood, spend their days alone with their children shielding them against the rest of the world and doing so in the most implacable and authoritarian way possible.

The only logical solution to this problem would be to abandon children on some desert island – but Rousseau thought of that. Assuming that they were able to survive, we would still have to have the most backward notion of 'human nature' to believe that these noble savages far from 'the consumer society' would develop all the innate virtues, all the natural aspirations to generosity and unselfishness that society represses. In reality, these children would be neither noble nor ignoble in the way that people usually understand those words. They would forge ideas, feelings and values for themselves, dictated by nothing more than the material circumstances of their existence. And if they were subjected to the **prime** daily necessity of fighting for survival, they would consider any means of achieving that to be just – including violence to protect 'their' food or 'their' hunting grounds.

I have no intention of rewriting the history of humanity. The choice has to be posed in these terms: either we agree that children are odiously repressed by society, as we were before them; or we change society so that it no longer represses children. And if people really feel a deep need for revolt in the face of the 'infant human condition' – *and they do* – they must eventually realize that the causes of this condition lie in the organization of society, and thus that the only course is to overthrow that organization.

I realize that the majority of those who try out the communal experiment are convinced of the need for the revolution 'in general terms'. They will retort: 'We know all that already. We don't claim to be destroying capitalism in setting up communes, but if we are to create the revolution we just have to make an *initial* break with the dominant ideology in certain key areas. Children are an integral part of the revolution. We can't say, "First, we must make the revolution, and then we'll think about the children." '

And they'd be right! The need to break with the *status quo* is as urgent for children as it is for women or for anyone else. You could say that this need is so urgent that the one prerequisite of any revolution is to satisfy it. But that means precisely that we must *actively oppose* the bourgeoisie *now*, on various fronts.

Where children are concerned this means that, in the first place, women and teachers must see the young as a political force that stems from their rebellion against their specific experience of oppression. Let's apply ourselves to the task of providing the means of systematizing this rebellion and assisting its transition from an individualistic to a collective revolt. Let's apply ourselves to the task of helping to expose the roots of their subordination, so that they can progress from truancy to the struggle against the education system. Let's unite with them against our common enemies: the state machinery, for example, which takes them away from their parents not so much to free them from parental authority as to exercise its own authority directly. Let's demand that the responsible care of children should be wrested from the control of establishment specialists and the educational apparatus and put into the hands of parents and the children themselves. Let's stop treating children as incompetent, unable to grasp the significance of our ideas, and let's show them the reality of our society, so that they can understand the *other* forms of oppression that people suffer, and thus broaden and deepen their social awareness.

The history of all revolutionary movements demonstrates that children are capable of extraordinary political awareness. They are capable of rebellion not only against what oppresses them, but against everything that oppresses the people. They are moved to boundless enthusiasm by just causes. Witness the daily examples of Indochina, the Middle East, Black America and Ireland.

How could we doubt it? After all in 1968 we in France saw thirteen-year-olds organize collective teams to look after the younger children so that their parents could occupy a factory. We saw schoolchildren fighting alongside students and workers on the barricades in May 1968, and organizing action committees in which the average age was sometimes under thirteen. More recently we have seen first-formers in the secondary school at Hurst fight like tigers for their teacher to be reinstated – a fight which created a panic in the Departments of the Interior and Education. For once, as one of those first-formers said, they had a teacher who respected them, who told them about life and reality. Obviously this rebellion cannot happen spontaneously – otherwise it would have happened before.

In the first place, children must be involved in extensive and repeated inquiries into the direction their studies should take. Women, as children's first teachers, must resolutely apply themselves to that task – they have a very important *role to play in this*. We women must be convinced that *we are not only repressed, but also repressing*. As long as we deny our role, even if we don't deliberately choose it, we shall never be able to understand kids' aspirations or to help them. A woman who oppresses a child will never be able to free herself. If they are to be emancipated themselves women must help children to become emancipated – their fates are inextricably linked.

Clearly, as you can guess, I do not claim to set out a 'programme' here. Anyhow, what would be the aim behind it? Everything remains to be done: inquiries, experiments, struggles, debates and studies. And they must be somewhat more specific than what I've done here. The ideas that I've expressed here may be mine alone, and may even be quite mistaken. And yet, in the last analysis, that doesn't matter much. They will be criticized and that's a good thing for a start. In discussing the topic of children in China and all the questions which have a bearing on it, I've tried to show that, far from losing sight of the concerns of women's emancipation, this attempt to understand the problems of child-rearing and education has kept us at the centre of our subject.

Part Four
THE CHINESE FAMILY: TOWARDS A NEW GRASS-ROOTS COLLECTIVITY

Introduction

At the risk of agreeing with the journalistic scaremongers who excel in telling tales about 'the Chinese nightmare', we must accept that the family may have been destroyed in China. If by family we understand a wife's submission to her husband, a wife's isolation in the home, the absolute authority of parents over children; if by family we designate that secluded 'haven of peace' which is the ideal of all men and without which life has no meaning, that little island over which the husband rules and for which he struggles, by means of wit and cunning, alone against the problems of daily life – yes, that family has all but disappeared! In the preceding chapters we have seen a China in which familial roles and structure, both actual and supposed, have not just been shaken, but have actually been eradicated or replaced by other forms of organization.

At the same time the whole truth might disillusion others. And the whole truth is that a kind of family does exist in China – if by family we understand a monogamous and stable couple whose children live with them; children who, apparently, will have no sexual experiences outside the family they in turn will set up later. This family is a saddening sight to a section of the revolutionary movement. But the question isn't quite so simple and deserves closer examination. If we can show that the family has been destroyed and yet still survives, then surely what we refer to by the term 'family' is more confused than we might at first think?

9 A Historical Survey

No one would think of purely and simply identifying feudal polygamy with what convention describes as the nuclear family of our society. But these two family types do have one striking feature in common: the woman's inferiority in her relationship with her husband. It's as impossible to imagine a feudal society based on small-scale agricultural production with a structure of cell-like families consisting of couples and their children, as it would be to find a capitalist society composed of broadly, based families in which the father and his wives and his wives' children and his wives' nubile sisters and his parents and their parents would all live together. Because, as we know, the different forms of family are *products* of different societies and are suited to the ends of those societies (not always exactly, but we'll come back to that later).

The Chinese family has one historical peculiarity, and it's one of the most important for increasing our understanding of the different functions of different types of families. In the space of barely twenty-five years China changed from a society of feudal families to one with a type of family that isn't known in any capitalist country. This rapid and recent development is important, because it's the only thing that can help us to understand a number of special aspects of the Chinese women's movement. As a result we can better discover which elements in the contemporary Chinese family *might be* of universal applicability.

Blood wedding
We heard many stories in China. One told us of the life of a peasant woman from the Sin Kiang Mountains whose feet had been bound and mutilated to make them small. Another was told to us by a woman working on the Red Flag Canal, who, almost smiling and in measured tones, related how, at the age of eight, she used to be whipped daily by her stepfather. Another was told by a young Tibetan woman sitting in a deep armchair with a long and brightly coloured dress hiding her legs, who couldn't stop crying when she recalled the landowner whose serf she was, and the day he caught her trying to escape, tied her feet to his horse's tail and dragged her back at a gallop, her head and back bouncing on the stone road. All these

stories merge into one tale of horrendous misery – the life of one woman indistinguishable from the lives of all the rest. The daughters of the poor were not by any means gifts from heaven to their families. The lucky parents were those who could arrange an early betrothal, since the girl would then be the responsibility of her future in-laws. In exchange for food and lodging – and beatings – she would serve her fiancé's parents from dawn to dusk – a most practical arrangement! Later on she would give her husband sons, and with a little luck she could inflict on her daughter-in-law the same treatment as she had received herself.

What could be worse than the condition of women in a feudal family? Everything can be done to them – they can be bought, sold, beaten, raped and sacrificed to the gods; have their feet bound and mutilated and their children stolen from them. The reality of these women's lives is unimaginable.

Their whole life would echo with the rule of the three obediences: obedience to their father when young; obedience to their husband when married; obedience to their eldest son when widowed.

And yet things didn't always go smoothly, and arranged marriages could often be organized only by the use of force:

'It wasn't a question of being willing or not. Of course anyone would have protested. But they just tied her up with a rope, stuffed her into the bridal chair, carried her to the man's house, forced her to put on the bridal head-dress, performed the ceremony in the hall and locked them into their room; and that was that. But Hsiang Lin's wife is quite a character. I heard she really put up a great struggle, and everybody said it must be because she had worked in a scholar's family that she was different from other people. Madam, I've seen a great deal. When widows remarry, some cry and shout, some threaten to commit suicide, some when they have been carried to the man's house won't go through the ceremony, and some even smash the wedding candlesticks. But Hsiang Lin's wife was different from the rest. They said she shouted and cursed all the way, so that by the time they had carried her to Ho village she was completely hoarse. When they dragged her out to the chair, although two men and her younger brother-in-law used all their strength, they couldn't force her to go through the ceremony. The moment they were careless enough to loosen their grip – Gracious Buddha! She threw herself against a corner of the table and knocked a big hole in her head. The blood poured out and although they used two handfuls of incense ashes and bandaged her with two pieces of red cloth, they still couldn't stop the bleeding. Finally it took all of them together to get her shut up with her husband in the bridal chamber, where she went on cursing. Oh it was really . . .' She shook her head and said no more. [1]

It's obvious that there were some husbands-to-be who never actually became husbands – even when they relied on force. Some fiancées would kill themselves rather than marry. And this wasn't a rare occurrence. In 1919, during the mass rising of Chinese revolutionary youth, the suicide of a young woman named Chao stirred women's anger against forced marriage.

The three iron cables

... A suicide is determined entirely by the environment. Was Miss Chao's original intention to die? No, it was not. On the contrary, it was to live. Yet her final decision to die was forced by her environment. Miss Chao's environment consisted in the following: one, Chinese society; two, the Chao family of Nanyang street, Changsha; and three, the Wu family of Kantzuyuan, Changsha, the family of the man she did not want to marry. These three factors formed three iron cables which one can imagine as a sort of three-cornered cage. Once confined by these three iron cables, no matter how she tried, there was no way in which she could stay alive. The opposite of life is death, and so Miss Chao died ... If one of these factors had not been an iron cable, or if she had been set free from the cables, then Miss Chao surely would not have died.

First, if Miss Chao's parents had not forced her and had allowed Miss Chao the freedom of her own will, then Miss Chao surely would not have died. Second, if Miss Chao's parents had not used force in this matter, and if they had allowed her to make known her views to her future in-laws, and to explain the reasons for her refusal, and if, in the end, her future in-laws had complied with her wishes and respected her individual freedom, then surely Miss Chao would not have died. And third, even if neither her parents nor her future in-laws had granted her free will, had there been in society a powerful source of public opinion to support her, and had there been some new world where the fact of having run away to seek refuge elsewhere was considered honourable and not dishonourable, then surely Miss Chao would not have died. For today Miss Chao had died because she was rigidly confined by the three iron cables (society, her parents and her future in-laws). Having sought in vain for life, in the end she sought death ...

Yesterday's event was a major one, and its circumstances were the rotten marriage system, the benighted social system and thought which could not be independent and love which could not be free ... The family of the parents and the family of the future in-laws both belong to society. They both constitute a proportion of society. We must realise that while both the family of the parents and the family of prospective in-laws have perpetrated a crime, the sources of the crime exist in society. While these two families could have committed the crime themselves, the larger part of their guilt was transmitted to them by society. Moreover, if society were good, and they themselves had wanted to perpetrate this crime, they would not have been able to do so ...

If we launch a campaign for the reform of the marriage system, we must first destroy all superstitions regarding marriage, of which the most important is destruction of belief in 'predestined marriage'. Once this belief has been abolished, all support for the policy of parental arrangement will be undermined and the notion of the 'incompatibility between husband and wife' will immediately appear in society. Once a man and wife demonstrate incompatibility, the army of the family revolution will arise *en masse* and a great wave of freedom of marriage and freedom of love will break over China[2]

This is an excerpt from an article written by Mao Tse-tung in 1919. Mao draws a close parallel betwe between the struggle against the 'man-eating' society and the struggle against arranged marriages. The principle of forced marriage was even opposed by some men – those who had been married at the age of seven or eight didn't value the custom at all. Sometimes they too would attempt to escape their fate and flee from their villages. Most of these men went to swell the ranks of the People's Liberation Army.

THE GREAT UPHEAVAL

There could be no solution for women in feudal China. Their oppression wasn't just maintained by ancient customs, or by the weight of age-old traditions. The oppression of married women was wholly the product of an economic system. Otherwise how are we to understand the survival of such a situation for a period of only a few years, let alone for centuries. Throughout her long history China has known many peasant revolts, but peasants have never triumphed and women have never been able to glimpse another way of living. It wasn't until the proletariat appeared on the scene that a new road emerged with a light at the end of it for hundreds of millions of peasants, and for women. That is why the Chinese Women's Liberation Movement is so closely linked with the revolution. For the first time ever women could envisage a new role for themselves on earth and the possibility of doing something other than serving their husbands, serving their mothers-in-law, serving the landowners and serving the gods. For the first time ever they could envisage the possibility of leaving their place by the fireside, on the *k'ang*[3] or at the well. 'The freedom of love will spread all over China!' was a sentiment that had little to do with reality for hundreds of millions of women. A popular Chinese song sums up their feelings:

> There was a girl of seventeen
> Four years hence at twenty-one
> She wed a boy of ten
> By eleven years the younger one!
>
> Her husband clung to her skirts
> As she fetched water from the well
> (One side was low, the other high)
> She said 'Away!' in case he feared he fell.
>
> 'If my in-laws weren't so kind
> I would throw you in the water
> If my in-laws wouldn't mind
> I would throw you in, my husband,' says this daughter.

A woman wanting to leave might well have heard her husband say, 'What would you do without me? Who would feed you? Who would till the fields for you? You're acting like a scatterbrained woman, dreaming up idle fantasies. You've got no alternative, though. You're destined to serve me here, just as I'm destined to serve the landowners who are graced with manna from heaven.'

Women's liberation could never have been the concern of women *alone*. Too much was involved in their oppression and they depended on so many 'props'. It could have happened only within the revolution, in the same way as the revolution couldn't have taken place without people doing away with superstitions, respect for the clan, ancestor worship and the matrimonial power structure, all of which upheld the landowners' autocracy. That's why the women's movement spread so rapidly in the areas liberated by the Red Army of workers and peasants. Women in all these areas took over the 'great upheaval' and by the time the Eighth Route Army arrived they were well on the way to persuading themselves that equality between men and women could be achieved. And so they organized teams to discover typical cases of families in which the women were treated particularly badly. They would go and see such a woman, talk to her and try to persuade her that if women were united, she would be able to shake off her yoke. Then they would arrange meetings for all the women in the village and summon the husband or the father-in-law to defend himself publicly against the accusations made by the woman or the daughter-in-law. If he refused to answer they would often give him a beating to show him that things would be different from now on and that he had better not abuse the woman once he was alone with her. The women's committee would be present, ever-watchful and ready to intervene again if necessary. Hinton writes.

Among those who were beaten was poor peasant Man-ts'ang's wife. When she came home from a Women's Association meeting, her husband beat her as a matter of course, shouting, 'I'll teach you to stay home. I'll mend your rascal ways.' But Man-ts'ang's wife surprised her lord and master. Instead of staying home thereafter as a dutiful chattel, she went the very next day to the secretary of the Women's Association, militiaman Ta-hung's wife, and registered a complaint against her husband. After, in a discussion with the members of the executive committee, the secretary called a meeting of the women of the whole village. At least a third, perhaps even half of them, showed up. In front of this unprecedented gathering of determined women a demand was made that Man-ts'ang explain his actions. Man-ts'ang, arrogant and unbowed, readily complied. He said that he beat his wife because she went to meetings and 'the only reason women go to meetings is to gain a free hand for flirtation and seduction'.

This remark aroused a furious protest from the women assembled before him. Words soon led to deeds. They rushed at him from all sides, knocked him down, kicked him, tore his clothes, scratched his face, pulled his hair and pummelled him until he could no longer breathe. 'Beat her, will you? Beat her, and slander us all, will you? Well, rape your mother. Maybe this will teach you.'

'Stop, I'll never beat her again,' gasped the panic-stricken husband who was on the verge of fainting under their blows.

They stopped, let him up, and sent him home with a warning – let him so much as lay a finger on his wife again and he would receive more of the same 'cure'.

From that day onward Man-ts'ang never dared beat his wife and from that day onwards his wife became known to the whole village by her maiden name, Ch'eng Ai-lien, instead of simply by the title of Man-ts'ang's wife, as had been the custom since time began. [4]

This is how the 'great upheaval' (as the women call it) was brought about, and even if husbands weren't always quick to approve of their wives' social involvement, they soon learned caution. It was generally true that the Women's Association went through this first stage in order to ensure the minimum security necessary for those women who wanted to join in the struggle.

FOR EACH CLASS ITS OWN KIND OF FAMILY

While forced marriage, and in particular the buying and selling of child-brides, was common to the whole of Chinese society and pointed to the generally inferior position of women, there were noticeable differences between noble and poor families.

Among the Han nation, who constitute 90 per cent of the Chinese people, polygamy had been illegal for a long time. But concubinage was quite legitimate. A man could marry and still have the right to as many concubines as he wished, and he could take them into his conjugal home. Concubines had the same duties as a legal wife. In particular, they owed respect and obedience to the head of the household. But they didn't have the same rights. They also had to obey the legal wife. While the legal wife belonged to the same social class as her husband – and wasn't chosen by him, but through a family agreement, without his or her consent – concubines almost always came from the poorer classes, and wee were chosen by their 'user' himself. In most cases they would be thrown out when they got too old or fell ill or when, for whatever reason, they were no longer 'up to the job'. There was little they could then do – except to swell the ranks of the army of beggars and vagabonds or try to hire themselves out as servants in a rich family. Although any children they might have had were legally entitled to the same rights as legitimate children, in reality they were often exploited by the master as simple farmhands. Daughters would suffer just about the same fate as their mothers, becoming concubines in their turn to other lords. They could occasionally hope to become legitimate wives, but generally of a poor husband. Their lives would be left in the hands of the master, to shape them as he pleased. Of course there were exceptions. Sometimes the child of a concubine would become the master's legal heir, if, for example, the wife had been unable to continue the line – in particular if she had failed to provide a male heir. But recognition of a concubine's child was a positive disadvantage to her, since from that moment on the child was lost to her and became the child of the legal couple.

The lord would select and purchase his concubines from poor families. They had no say in the matter of course, and very often their daughters' only chance of survival was to be sold to the lord. Sometimes the sale of a daughter would raise some money to support her brothers and sisters for a little longer. Sometimes a family up to its ears in debt to the lord would give their daughter away as a 'deposit' – no transaction would take place, but in his ineffable goodness the lord and master would consent to defer the payment of debts until the next harvest.

Quite clearly this *de facto* polygamy was restricted to wealthy men, who had the power to get what they wanted when they wanted it. It was very different for poor men. Far from being polygamous, they were often forced to remain single because they couldn't afford a wife. Among some of the national minorities the law clearly sanctioned different family structures for different social classes. For example serf-owners in Tibet were legally polygamous – and this didn't exclude concubinage. However, serfs were required to practise monogamy, which was a sign of poverty. Serf marriages were decided exclusively by the landowner, who wished his serfs to have descendants, since he would have proprietary rights over them, too. Polyandry was practised in distant corners of Tibet and among even poorer sections of the serf class. In the Peking Institute for National Minorities we were told that this kind of polyandry should not be understood as a straight female equivalent to polygamy. The women didn't choose several husbands, but rather several men were obliged to share one wife because they were too poor to aspire to one each.

These different family structures, whether written into the law – as in Tibet – or contingent on material circumstances – as with the Han nation – indicate where each family type is placed within the social structure. But to see how family types are organized *as a whole* according to the social structure in which they function is only a starting-point. We have yet to learn to recognize how a given family type (or structure) functions within its social class in one society. For the mass of the poor peasantry, dependent on small-scale private production with no resources other than their land and labour power, a family was the only chance of survival. A wife to share the work-load was an absolute imperative for the peasant – he would farm the land while she went about small-scale domestic production. As long as China had a tiny industrial output, the peasant's wife and daughters bore the responsibility for making clothes, preserving food and providing all short-term family needs, while the sons provided vital long-term security for the peasant's old age. With no children the peasant would inevitably die of hunger and cold.

For the landowner, enriched by the fruits of the work of others, a family meant something altogether different. First and foremost it was the medium of inheritance – the thing that enabled property to be handed down from generation to generation, maintaining wealth and power in the hands of the same restricted group of people and the same despotic class. Concubinage was part of the same scheme: the larger the number of his descendants the broader the landowner's power base. Second, a large family – wife, concubines, children – and a retinue of servants (over whom he had the *droit de seigneur,* as he did over all the daughters of the local poor) was, simultaneously, the *symbol and instrument* of his control over the local people. Taking concubines from among the lower peasantry also meant that 'sacred' familial bonds were created between the landowner and the peasants. Of course these bonds put the landowner under no kind of obligation to the girl's parents, but they did ensure that peasant superstitions and religious beliefs against harming kinfolk or their property were reinforced. Thus family types differed according to the different needs and functions of the individual family in each social class.

THE DEMOCRATIC FAMILY

The step-by-step destruction of the ancient economic and political functions of the family

The Marriage Law of 1950, passed on the morrow of the liberation, is evidence of the changes in male–female relations that came in with the new democratic revolution. Bigamy and concubinage were forbidden. Marriage for boys or girls under eighteen was also prohibited. Mutual consent became the only basis for marriage. The grounds for divorce were no longer restricted and divorce itself could be obtained free of charge.

But this was only the law, sanctioning the end of feudal *mores* and indicating a new political direction. The ancient family functions still had to be eliminated in practice. Agrarian reform, in destroying the great estates, dealt a fatal blow to the old family structures. The redistribution of land among the peasant families, and also among all women living on their own or wanting to leave their husbands, considerably undermined the power of the institution of marriage. An enormous wave of divorces swept China in the ensuing period and many arranged marriages were dissolved.

Conjugal love, which was never even alleged to be a basis for marriage, now became a sufficient justification for it. And the aspirations of Chinese youth, which Mao Tse-tung had supported thirty years earlier (see the text on Miss Chao's suicide above), were fulfilled in part. In his analysis of the role of love in marriages in different societies, Engels had this to say about societies where forced marriages were customary: 'Throughout antiquity marriages were arranged by the parents; the parties quietly acquiesced. The little conjugal love that was known to antiquity was not in any way a subjective inclination, but an objective duty; not a reason for but a correlate of marriage.' [5] which sums up rather well the Chinese situation before the revolution. With freedom of marriage, '... a new moral standard arises for judging sexual intercourse. The question asked is not only whether such intercourse was legitimate or illicit, but also whether it arose from mutual love or not.' [6]

And that is also the significance of the Chinese laws which followed the liberation. Commenting in 1950 on the Marriage Law, Teng Ying-chao (Chou Enlai's wife) specifically argued that the struggle for fair implementation of the law must rest on the following points:

First, the cadres should study the Marriage Law and remould their ideology in order to eliminate the remnant feudal ideology that man is superior to woman and that women are playthings ... Second, organisations at all levels of the Party, of the Government, and of the people should earnestly conduct widespread and penetrating educational and propaganda campaigns among the people, so as to transform the opposition to the feudal marriage system into a broad movement of the masses. The Central Committee of the Party has made the statement that the whole Party should 'make the publicity and organisational work guaranteeing the correct carrying out of the Marriage Law one of its important and regular tasks at the present time ... Third, the *social freedom between men and women and the freedom to fall in love between unmarried men and women should be promoted*. There's no denying that an unhealthy point of view in this respect still exists in the minds of some of our cadres. More often than not gossiping runs riot when a man comrade becomes friendly with a woman comrade. We should oppose such an attitude. *We must provide the proper social environment for the carrying out of the Marriage Law*. It must be pointed out here that love and marriage are the private affairs of individuals and should not be interfered with by others, and, if viewed more positively, they are part of the make up of social life. The smooth course of love and marriage of an individual is essential to a satisfactory social life. [7]

It's clear that Teng's first step served only to destroy feudal attitudes and further steps were necessary [8] before the situation so familiar to us – that of the family as unit of production – could be ended. In that situation, the transformation that must take place is no longer *predominantly* concerned with smashing feudalism (feudal structures have long since disappeared in the West), but with destroying bourgeois forms of the family. Of course China retains some individual characteristics. In the first place, the struggle against the bourgeois family structure is taking place under the aegis of a proletarian leadership. In the second place, the recent feudal past influenced the type of family structure set up during the progress of the New Democratic Revolution. Given all that, we enter an area clearly more familiar to us, the struggle against the bourgeois forms of the family.

Just as agrarian reform had dealt a fatal blow to the family structures of feudalism, so collectivization was to be a powerful factor in the disintegra-

A HISTORICAL SURVEY 117

tion of bourgeois structures of the family under the new democracy. The bourgeoisie understood this very well, and in suggesting a return to family-based production it tried to aim a precise blow against collectivization. To talk about 'a revolution in social relations' or about 'the necessary equality between the sexes' or about 'love as the foundation of free marriage' is easy; but as long as production is based on private property it is no more than empty phrase-mongering. The fact of inheritance of land or capital is, of itself and without any corresponding legal status, *enough* to make an economic necessity out of the family and a simple *contract of work* out of marriage. Women understood this particularly well, as we saw in the discussion of the struggle against Liu Shao-chi's policy of the Zhen Zui YiBao.

For all that, the family as an economic edifice was only shaken, not levelled to the ground. The family remained for some time the chief repository of too many of its former functions, like child care, housework and the care of the retired. Before marriage could be freed from its traditional material constraints, further steps had to be taken. The collectivization of housework on a grand scale had to be got under way, while certain duties that were previously familial (such as health or responsibility for retired workers) were being socialized.

10 Leisure Time, Work Time

We were often told during our visit that Chinese men and women are today economically, politically and legally equal. This was obviously meant to suggest that women are not discriminated against in any way and that the contrary, as we shall see later, may even be true. Now complete equality between men and women should lead to an equal distribution of both sexes in all sectors of society. Yet there are still many areas with a majority of men, and some areas almost exclusively reserved for women. If you look, for example, at the structure of the leadership you will find that the ratio of women to men in positions of power is markedly low, and that the higher you look in the power structure, the lower it will be (see appendix). This is a real sign that equality doesn't exist in practice, and indeed it couldn't yet be otherwise.

Recognizing that sexual inequality still persists, even though the subject may be passed over in silence, is nevertheless an important first step. Sometimes the inequality of women was presented to us as a simple 'retardation' due to the remnants of inherited ideas: 'We must struggle against the reactionary ideas about women's inferiority that are left over from the past.' But to say *only* that much is to keep silent about the contemporary material foundations on which relative inferiority still rests. The least difficult thing is to be absolutely convinced of the falsity of the ideas that have supported the inferior status of women. But to achieve real equality it is essential to destroy the material obstacles in its path. Unless these obstacles are exposed — and this is a prerequisite for their destruction — such equality will never be attained. To point to the material base underlying the inferiority of Chinese women is an indispensable political task — not only for Chinese women and for the Chinese revolution, but for all women and for the world revolution.

We have already seen how housework is still undergoing a continuing process of socialization. With this socialization as yet incomplete, the family unit has to bear some of the responsibility for providing for its members. This domestic work is, of course, part of the material base which reproduces the family as an economic unit — even if the family's responsibility in this area is constantly diminishing. And privatized domestic work is a *material* and not an ideological obstacle to the full emancipation of women.

Replacing capitalist ownership of the means of production by collective ownership under socialism is not a simple legislative measure. The proletariat cannot, on seizing power, simply decree the end of the capitalist base. This notion of socialism by decree, which is still widely held, is simply a variation on the revisionist theme, in which all the material foundations of capitalism appear as worthy of preservation, with the sole exception of the legal structure of ownership. In this account of socialism, nationalized enterprises and joint-stock companies which aren't the private property of a single flesh-and-blood boss appear as models of the new order. What a great communist Napoleon must have been, to decree the nationalization of the tobacco trade! [1] As we shall see, these judicial illusions have implications for the women's movement.

'Wherever' "capitalism as such" has been destroyed, the oppression of women is attributed to purely ideological causes, implying a non-Marxist and idealist definition of ideology as a factor that can subsist in the absence of the material oppression which it helps rationalize.' [2] But what does the destruction of 'capitalism as such', mean if it doesn't mean that the socialist phase has been completed and communism has been achieved? Socialism doesn't entail the disappearance of capitalism and the removal of every material condition on which relationships of oppression and inequality depend. To believe that it does is neither more nor less than to imagine that 'old ideas' surviving without a material base bear the sole responsibility for all oppression and inequality still existing under socialism. It comes back to the claim that communism and socialism have the same material base, and differ only in that communist ideology is appropriate to that base, while socialism is saddled with the ideology of the past.

Throughout the socialist phase, capitalism and communism, each represented by its social class, are locked in a ruthless struggle. Wherever capitalism is defeated embryonic communist relations are created, but as long as capitalism is dominant in whole sectors of society, communism will not be established.

Suppose there was a revolution in France today. This very evening, the proletariat decrees the abolition of capitalist ownership of the means of production. Will it then have destroyed 'capitalism as such'? Certainly not. The division between manual and intellectual work will still remain, the wage system won't have been abolished. It takes more to build communism than a single stroke of the pen, just as it takes more than a single round of machine-gun fire to destroy capitalism. The proletariat cannot *escape the legacy* of the capitalist division between manual and intellectual work – a division that is essential to capitalism and has been taken by it to incredible extremes. And as long as one capitalist relation exists, capitalism itself still exists.

The destruction of the division between manual and intellectual work necessitates a profound revolution in education and a continuous upheaval in the social relations of production. Inside the factories manual workers will no longer work with their hands alone and intellectuals will no longer be pure minds. Under the political leadership of manual workers both will strive to create the new man who is both manual worker and intellectual. That is the task that China has specifically undertaken, by every means possible, not least by means of the Cultural Revolution. Good intentions alone will never achieve the goal. Only a continued struggle will destroy 'capitalism as such'.

The same applies to the oppression of women. Where it persists under socialism, even if it has been weakened, this isn't because socialism 'as such' provides a material base for this oppression, or because the oppression of women is beyond social oppression, but solely because 'capitalism as such' hasn't been completely eradicated.

THE WAGE SYSTEM AND THE OPPRESSION OF WOMEN

The fact that wage earning still exists in China, although it is very different from the wage system in the capitalist countries, means that labour-power is still a commodity that can be bought and sold – a situation that is alien to communism. The family will no longer be an economic unit *in any way,* and thus will no longer be a base of women's oppression, on the day, and only on that day, when the quantity or quality of labour expended by an individual will no longer have any bearing on his remuneration; 'to each according to his needs!'

There will no longer be any connection between work done and the satisfaction of needs; no standard by which to measure the one against the other. Work will cease to be a means of earning your daily bread and will become, in and of itself, the foremost of life's necessities, the richest and freest activity ever known to man. This state of affairs won't happen tomorrow, and as long as it is still to come, labour-power will remain a commodity in private hands – the one resource every individual owns. This commodity is therefore fashioned to suit the prevailing mode of production in society. It is not reproduced according to the wishes of the worker, but according to the requirements of production. As long as labour-power remains a commodity, the family necessarily remains a small factory for producing this commodity.

While the recent debates about wages in China may have tackled many issues other than the question of equal pay for women (see pp. 22-24), women themselves are still central to the arguments. After all, what is really in question is the continuation of the wage system.

The Cultural Revolution saw an important development in the march towards communism. The people joined in massive criticism of all the material incentives, production bonuses and wage differentials that seemed designed to divide them. But from then on a new divisive notion was established. Differentiation on the grounds of quality became the main element in the wage system. And qualitative judgements were made not just on the technical level, but on a political level, too – how committed a worker's attitude was and how collective his work was were the new criteria for remuneration. That's all very well, but is rewarding a progressive political attitude with higher pay any improvement on the old capitalist system of material incentives? Shouldn't we question the monetary valuation of revolutionary political attitudes which specifically attack the capitalist idea of work? 'Working for money, to earn a living' will be replaced in the revolutionary canon by 'Working for the people, without gain and without financial return'. The principle of rewarding political attitudes must surely transform the evolution of vanguard ideas among the mass into the evolution of the vanguard into an élite? The principle of rewarding political attitudes must surely run the risk of producing political careerists who will always toe the party line and benefit from doing so. It must surely also run the risk of gradually replacing collectivist consciousness by individualistic display, since a political attitude has to be noticed if it is to be appreciated and *rewarded*. All this involves the obvious danger of an inflation of external signs of revolutionary spirit. And this is quite the reverse of what is wanted.

While the above shows that destroying the old system of rewards does present problems, similar problems arise with the progressive introduction of a new system for providing for people's needs. To deny that there are unequal situations, and hence unequal needs (in health, housing or the size of a family, for example), and to consider only the labour a worker expends, also maintains a form of capitalist wage earning. These inequalities must be taken into account, and attempts must be made to eliminate them step by step. The problem seems to have been solved in some places by giving an income supplement to those in greater need. But does that constitute any kind of step towards the progressive elimination of wage earning? No, it clearly reinforces the wage system. It is not a question of choosing between 'denying the existence of different needs resulting from inequalities' on the one hand, and 'providing income supplements' on the other. The real choice is between 'denying different needs as a fact of capitalism' and 'creating collective forms that reduce these inequalities, not by increasing salaries, but by ensuring that society takes over direct responsibility for fulfilling needs.'

Whenever a worker's wife' with children falls ill, taking the family's needs into account doesn't mean increasing the worker's wages. Rather it means a crèche to look after the smallest child night and day for as long as necessary; a service team bringing cooked meals to the house; the district health team taking care of the sick woman; free medical treatment; and, if necessary, the provision by the neighbourhood committee of financial aid for the family from the local *solidarity* fund. It means keeping the husband's morale up and making the sick woman feel that she's not forgotten. It means surrounding the children with affection. It means the spirit of comradely help and warmth from the neighbours, from the old

people's committee, the women's committee, the school, the crèche, the factory and the hospital. And there isn't a going rate for that!
Western society is organized in such a way that each individual can rely on no one but himself and his family to survive, no matter what difficulties arise. In the West, the morality of the market-place and the principle of bourgeois equality amount to this: 'You work for so many hours and you get paid accordingly. It makes no difference whether you have five children or none at all, whether you are in good health or on your death bed, whether you have a home or live in a shanty town.' In China the socialist principle of 'he who doesn't work doesn't eat' is applied only to point out in clear terms that no one has the right to live off another's labour. But nothing material or ideological is denied the sick worker or the worker with special problems.

Finally, and most importantly, since work is no longer purely the expenditure of labour-power, labour-power itself is no longer merely the sum total of greater or lesser physical or psychological capacities. The production of new labour-power thus tends to be less and less a matter of its daily reproduction, of the simple business of eating and sleeping to be on form tomorrow. It tends more and more to take shape in the workers' increasing knowledge of diverse techniques, of new technologies and of society itself.

The worker is not pushed to fulfil quotas; he or she is expected to participate in working out new projects and techniques; to take factory study courses or go to university; to become a barefoot doctor; to run educational establishments; to learn about military matters; to participate in the industrialization of rural areas; to be an artist, a poet, a philosopher; and, above all, actively and consciously to further the revolution. What do the 'capacities' of this worker and those of the proletarian figure of capitalism, mutilated and enslaved in the service of machines, have in common?

A comparison between the situation of workers in the West and that of their Chinese counterparts, whose work is so much broader in scope, highlights another function of the family under capitalism: to crystallize the worker's free time and force him or her to 'put up with' the time he or she spends in work. The unnatural separation between leisure time and work time is typical of an exploitative society which sees the sole significance of work as enabling you to earn enough to survive.

The proletarian, *dispossessed of everything,* can only carry out an endless ritual of fragmented and senseless operations, bored to death and expending great physical effort, for as long as it takes to make a living. We work to earn a living, but what kind of life are we working for? [3] Take away the time spent earning and we are left with free time – the time in which all our hopes, all our aspirations are placed. The days of rest seem like the only possible moments of real existence; home the only possible place where we can live the good life; and holidays the only possible goal of the whole year. At least, these are the daydreams of our working life. In these conditions it is no surprise to find that 'private life' is so important to us. A car, a telly, a little 'home of our own', all spick and span, foster the illusion of a flight away from this hated society. And to escape means to have leisure. And leisure is filled with the family. Without a family and without the need to support it, nothing in the world could force a worker to labour in the conditions he now works in. The capitalist employer would have to resort to the violence of the slave owner if it weren't for the family. Craftsmen and poor peasants were also compelled to work in order to survive – that isn't an invention of capitalism. Yet the craftsman had control over the manner of his production. He was simultaneously an intellectual conceiving a project and a worker making it with his own hands. His labour therefore had a significance which enriched a working life whose physical boundaries were the four walls of his workshop. And even that was immeasurably more fulfilling labour than his children would experience, when vast industries came to ruin the craftsman, to deprive him of his tools and to replace his hard-won skills by assembly-line techniques of slavery, tightening up bolts or patching up the paintwork on a car body.[4] Of course the solution isn't to return to the hallowed days of the artisan. Indeed capitalism was a progressive force when it shattered the partitions dividing one crafts from another and transcended the limited horizon of the journeyman – they were specialists in their own fields, but totally ignorant in all other fields. The creation of a proletariat with the capacity to think in universal terms and to sketch out an egalitarian society of integral human beings also represented progress. But this same proletariat will remain incapacitated as long as the means by which this vision will be realized are hidden, and as long as the vision itself is obscured. Momentarily deprived of revolutionary goals, life has no other meaning than the search for the illusory ideal of leisure. The oppressed place all their hope in the family. Their disappointment and bitterness are all the greater because they have invested their greatest dreams in the family.

When the gap between alienating work and escapist leisure begins to be bridged, inevitable changes in the family will follow. From being a pseudo-refuge, it becomes one fundamental collective among others, open to society and in a symbiotic relationship with it.

This is what the Chinese experience reveals. Nothing can be understood about the new Chinese family if it is seen outside the social transformation in which it is situated; if the place that each of its members is beginning to take in society is overlooked. Instead of thinking about Chinese men, women or children in the abstract, you must imagine a woman like Ma Yuyin from the Chao Yan factory – a woman who is fully aware, who is participating in the collective creation of a new life and helping to change the world so that she can transform herself. A woman like this, who leaves for her factory every morning to 'make the revolution', has little left in common with the housewives of our world, who, as Lenin said, '. . . continue to be "household slaves", for they are overburdened with the drudgery of the most squalid, backbreaking and stultifying toil in the kitchen and the family household'.[5] You must imagine a real child, little Li in the Nanking school, for example. A child aware of social reality and of what is at stake in the struggles to change the school; a child integrated into the world which is therefore, no longer the world of adults alone; a child who organizes with his friends the most varied activities imaginable – scientific experiments, medicine, debates on international politics, military training, the fromation of children's platoons and street sweeping. A child like that no longer has much in common with our children, those submissive and oppressed minors whom psychoanalysis has placed at the apex of the family triangle. You must imagine a real man, one of the millions of peasants, like a man who lives in Shawan, for example. This man is a farmworker and son of a farmhand. He organized the first mutual-aid team in Shawan and is now chairman of the revolutionary committee; he is still working in the fields with the others, still struggling against nature and class enemies to create a new world. This man to whom mending socks comes naturally, who sees looking after the children when his wife goes to study Marxism as a duty he owes her, is no longer an oppressed worker, or the male oppressor of our world. Such new women, children and men are no longer rare exceptions. They are prototype communists for all the people, representatives of the *direction of the revolution*. We must bear them in mind when we talk about the Chinese family – their new kind of labour and the new significance they've given it cuts across the family, modifying and liberating it.

11 The Idea of 'Nationalization' and its Fatal Consequences for the Family

OLD PEOPLE IN SOCIETY

No picture of the new Chinese family would be complete without some account of the place old people have in it. The Marriage Law stipulates that adults in good health must support their retired parents.[1] It must be understood, in this context, that retired workers receive a pension equivalent to about 80 per cent of their earnings. On the other hand, at the time of writing, peasants get no pension, and retirement age depends exclusively on their state of health. Generally they work less as they get older, tending to concentrate on less tiring jobs such as pig-breeding or rabbit-breeding and so on. As they work shorter hours they also earn less than adults in their prime. Clearly, the clause in the Marriage Law has an economic significance and guarantees that the family maintains one obvious economic function. If elderly peasants cannot support themselves, either totally or in part, the next generation of the family shoulders the whole responsibility for supporting them. This is true throughout the rural areas and is one of the aspects of the dichotomy that still exists between town and country. The Party's policy of lessening the differences has improved the lot of peasant families to a considerable extent. No doubt it's the development of the health service in rural areas that has resulted in the provision of all kinds of treatment for the old free of charge, for a nominal annual subscription of 2 yuans. Moreover, the setting up of numerous small clinics throughout China has prevented the old and the sick being isolated from their families in vast central hospitals. This is very different from the lamentable picture in our society — with old people virtually cut off from all emotional relationships, abandoned both by their relatives and by society, in the gloomy surroundings of a geriatric ward.

Collective restaurants and clothing workshops shoulder a good deal of the burden of the work that usually falls on the family caring for its old people. The constant improvement of the various collective services and the growth of productive forces should allow the society of the future to take full responsibility for meeting all the material needs of the older generation.

It would be a mistake to think that the young people look after the old just to fulfil a need arising from the present state of economic development. Even when old people to receive a pension enabling them to be self-sufficient, they still live with their children and grandchildren. This constant mixing of all ages in China, from infants to the elderly, has an obvious political significance.

Unlike his or her counterpart in the West, the elderly Chinese worker is not considered useless or a burden. The fusion of qualities from the old and young – political experience, born of years of practice in the class struggle, combined with enthusiasm and daring – results in an explosive mixture of great potency for the revolution.

Since the Cultural Revolution the social involvement of old people has further increased and widened in scope. The Old People's Committee of the city of Shanghai invited us to discuss this point with them. While on our way to their meeting-house in the middle of a block of flats, Noelle reminded us of the atmosphere of an old people's home like the one she had worked in. The home is like a hospital, the hospital is like a barracks; the barracks is like a prison. She spoke of the unbearable isolation of the spirit; the endless days spent in waiting, with nothing to wait for – except the letter that doesn't come, the meal that merely helps to pass the time, the Sunday visiting hour that brings no one, the hope that is never fulfilled, the ease of death.

The leader of the committee, elected by her comrades, was a short, wrinkled, white-haired woman. She wore a carefully ironed cotton jacket and trousers. Her name was Ho Yao-chen and she told us:

'Old age used to be at the same time a privilege and a great misfortune. A privilege, because the wretchedness of the people was such that life expectancy was very short and most of the poor died before reaching old age. A great misfortune because those who did survive were thrown out into the street as soon as they stopped being of use to the landowners and the capitalists ... Most people were often much too poor to be able to offer a home to their parents. Old people were either forced to sell their feeble strength, doing exhausting work for a derisory wage until they died or else they were reduced to begging from day to day, an existence beneath that of the animals. The victory of the revolution brought change, not least for us old people. Our society surrounds us with good-will; our health, welfare and happiness are paid unfailing attention. Our days are filled with sunshine under the dictatorship of the proletariat.'

The Cultural Revolution shook the attitudes of old people considerably. They quickly understood that only the continuation of the revolution could prevent the old society being resurrected. They joined in, writing and sticking up the city wall newspapers in which bourgeois pronouncements about the uselessness of the old were attacked. They took part in revolutionay meetings to work out revolutionary critiques; they conducted surveys in and around the city, so that they could become more aware of the people's

THE IDEA OF NATIONALIZATION 127

needs in order to run their activities for the success of the revolution. They organized teams of old people to do housework for the less able among them.

'Just because we now have enough money from our pensions to live without working is no reason to withdraw from the building of socialism,' a retired worker told us, to explain their own view of their activities. Many of those who are strong enough work a few hours a day in the service workshops, in the crèches or in the schools. They often spend their free time taking children round factories or hospitals, helping them with their investigations and, generally, helping them to acquire a class perspective. They arrange public exhibitions and meetings on the class struggle, to which they bring material or reminiscences about the old society. (We have already mentioned the active part played by old people in the schools, noting in particular their lessons on recent history as they experienced it.) Such activities in every sphere have the immediate result of integrating old people into the political life of the whole society. Comparatively recently the study of Marxism-Leninism has begun to play a substantial part in these activities. The committee told us that if old people didn't study revolutionary theory they wouldn't be able to learn the lessons of their long experience and transmit that invaluable understanding to the younger generations. Without doubt the extent of the politicization of the old can be gauged by the interest they take in the international situation.

It is a commonplace in the West to say that the horizons of the elderly are limited and that their lives consist of trivia. But this can be said only because society thrusts them aside and leaves them poverty-stricken like vegetables. Their fate has nothing natural about it; it is caused by the way society is organized.

One of the elderly Chinese said to us, 'How could we be preoccupied with trivial and ephemeral problems when three-quarters of mankind are still being exploited? When we take over some of the jobs in the neighbourhood we free forces for increasing production, not only for the Chinese people but also to help other nations in their struggle against imperialism. That's why we say that working in service workshops is a clear expression of the internationalism of old people.' This conquering state of mind is also reflected in the importance attached to physical fitness. We often saw old people doing gymnastics and we were told that most of them regularly take part in a variety of sports, and that there are frequent sports meetings between teams of old people.

After our discussion with the committee we listened to their choir. It was extremely moving to hear the 'Internationale' sung with such spirit and warmth, and by voices occasionally revealing the fragile and tremulous tones of old age. The role of old people and the esteem in which they are held have nothing in common with the lip-service we pay the old as a means of politely dismissing them and all their aspirations and activities without openly displaying contempt.

I had read an article in a Chinese periodical called 'An eighty-seven-year-old Tibetan woman is learning to read' with some curiosity. I confess to a feeling of scepticism about the interest that this effort could arouse. Knowing that it takes several years to learn enough Chinese characters to be able to read the newspapers, I thought: 'She's sure to die before she achieves her goal.' The article told the story of this woman's life. She was a former slave who had known only servitude, beatings and humiliation. She had worked all her life, literally chained to the kitchen, so oppressed by her owners that she had never even known an hour of relaxation sitting on the doorstep at midday, with the sun hovering high in the sky, sipping a cup of hot jasmin tea. – When asked, the old woman had said, 'Women today can learn and understand things. I want to be able to read.' How difficult we find it to shake off our market-place mentality, to stop calculating the return on everything we do! We are indeed heavily oppressed.

At this moment I can easily picture the white room where this old peasant woman tries to remember some large characters, drawn on a slate by a little girl. No one shows any surprise. This is not wasting time. Who is being educated? The former slave or the little girl?

This story is a perfect illustration of the point that what is at stake is not personal achievement through study, but the possibility that the underprivileged, oppressed and scorned masses may become the masters of the world. What difference does it make, in the last analysis, whether we talk of a woman on the eve of her death or of a child early in her life? In a society in which value is no longer calculated in terms of profit or as a return on investment, but is measured according to the sole criterion that what is right is what corresponds to the needs of the people, the *sine qua non* of our liberation, as individuals, as women, is the social principle.

If society was strictly divided into age groups, so that the old kept with the old and the young with the young, old people could never play the important part they do. This is one of the reasons why grass-roots collectives such as the family, where all the generations are united in communal practice, are so significant. And as long as old people are an integral part of all social activities and participate to the limit of their capacity, the family will be considerably enriched by their presence.

There are really only two possibilities for old people: either they are thought to have a vital role to play, and all material, ideological and political steps are taken to integrate them into all social activities; or they are thought to have outlived their social usefulness, and, depending on the wealth of the society and the extent of its 'barbarism', are either 'nationalized' in homes or abandoned to their own fate. The idea that *society* should take over from individual families in caring for those who can't look after themselves is often confused with the idea that the care of the old or the sick or the young is the *State's* responsibility. Old people's homes are put forward as indisputable evidence of social progress – especially by those who militate for the destruction of the family and venerate state control as *the* panacea for all ills. It's nothing of the sort! When a society is no longer driven by profit, when it no longer measures

THE IDEA OF NATIONALIZATION

productivity as a function of profitability, its relation to its formerly 'unproductive' members is radically altered. It doesn't give charity because its need for them is as great as their need for it. Putting their care totally into the hands of bureaucracy is to deny the irreplaceable usefulness of every member of society.

Those who believe in the idea of putting the old away and try to pass it off as a progressive theory lean heavily on the dichotomy between leisure time and work time that we mentioned earlier. 'They really do have the right to enjoy a rest after a lifetime of work.' 'They're entitled to have a bit of leisure now that they can no longer earn their living.' Retirement is then seen as the privileged period in a person's life – a period consisting of nothing but leisure. The reality, as Chinese society demonstrates, is otherwise. When social activities are experienced as free and enriching, you're not doing someone a favour by excluding him or her from them.

Of course this criticism of state care of the elderly is not meant to suggest that it would be fair to force each family to cope as best they can with their old people. It is right and proper that those who can no longer work should receive a pension ensuring their economic independence, and China is indisputably moving towards a situation of material autonomy for all her people. And I don't mean to suggest either that old people's homes should go. China, too, has a few homes for old people with no close relatives. But these homes aren't the only alternative open to such people. We were told that they would sometimes go and live with distant relatives, or even with families of friends who have no grandparents. Such arrangements would be subject to mutual consent – a kind of reverse, or rather reciprocal, adoption. Old people's homes are built inside housing estates and are open to everybody. Like anyone else, those who live there participate alone or with other old people in the estate's social life. But these homes are not put forward as prototypes of a new social institution.

ON ADOPTION

There are no orphanages in China – a fact which stresses the political significance the Chinese give to the question of institutional care. They believe that a revolutionary society must solve and surmount individual misfortune by means of class solidarity and the power of revolutionary commitment, not by administrative machinery.

'But what happens to children who have no parents?' we inquired, and we were told that this doesn't raise any particular problems. Such children are always adopted by grandparents, uncles, friends, or even neighbours. It's all very simple. If the children are still babies they will usually be adopted by relatives, even if they live far away. If they are already at school and have friends and emotional ties in the area, neighbours will usually adopt them. The wishes of the children are always taken into account in making this decision. The State pays a maintenance allowance for each orphan, and thus doesn't offload its financial responsibility onto the adoptive family. For it is thought preferable for orphans to live like other Chinese children, rather than being institutionalized.

We can fruitfully compare Chinese and western attitudes to child care by looking at a minor French scandal. A semi-skilled worker in a French car plant had lived for several years in an abandoned railway coach on a piece of waste ground with his wife and five children. In spite of numerous applications, he was never given a decent home. The wife fell seriously ill and was hospitalized for an indefinite time. The husband, who was on shift work, organized himself and his elder children to take over the mother's work in the home. The family, including a baby of a few months, looked after themselves like this for a few weeks. But then a social worker discovered their crisis situation while on a visit. The efficient and humane local administration, moved by this drama, took 'the necessary steps'. What do you think happened? Was a suitable home immediately provided for the family? Was an allowance given to the father so that he could pay for a full-time home help? Oh no! These are the dreams of incorrigible idealists. Administrative genius, in its infinite wisdom, dreamed up the proper solution. The father was left in his railway carriage. His five children were taken away from him – the younger ones were put into foster homes, the older ones were sent to boarding-schools run by the local authority. But if this seems too good to be true, you have yet to learn the full extent of administrative magnanimity. Great care was taken to send the baby to a wet nurse in Nevers; the two-year-old was specially selected for a foster-mother in Angers; the third child was sent north; the two eldest were placed in different schools in towns far apart! Ah, yes! The State had clearly fulfilled its obligations. The ladies of the idle rich no longer perform good works by caring for our social unfortunates. Nowadays the State will do it all with intelligence and sensitivity. And if the unfortunate worker is dissatisfied with the results if his eldest son runs away to rejoin the family, it can only be because the poor these days know only ingratitude, or sinister leftist ideas.

Chinese policy on adoption offers a clear contrast to the Soviet approach in the twenties. A law forbidding childless couples to adopt orphans or deserted children was introduced at the time, with the justification that such children were the State's responsibility. It was a logical measure, given the political goal of the destruction of the family that was then current. As we have seen, the Chinese hold a diametrically opposite view: abandoning children is forbidden by law and all orphans are adopted.

Weh Cheng and Chang Kua are brothers, aged eight and ten. Their parents, workers in Shanghai, died within a few months of one another. The children weren't on their own for long. Since they didn't want to leave their school, or their friends, the neighbours adopted them collectively. The State paid the necessary allowance to support them and they grew up as orphans among children with parents, but were carefully looked after by the other families. When winter came round, everyone would make sure

THE IDEA OF NATIONALIZATION 131

that they were properly dressed to go out. In the evenings they could eat in the district restaurant with other children or with a family. The collective responsibility didn't stop at making sure they were in good health. The old people's committee, in particular, often invited them to hear about life long ago in stories such as all grandfathers tell in China. Somebody had to make sure that they would get a class perspective on the past. The two brothers were never short of affection. There was never a family celebration to which they weren't invited. Everyone worried about their school work, everyone was interested in their pastimes. They were criticized, of course, but not with indulgent pity. Their relationships had all the warmth characteristic of a revolutionary society.

The law goes further than ensuring the adoption of orphans. Article 13 of the Marriage Law, dealing with the relationships between parents and children, forbids the desertion of children. 'Parents have the duty to rear and to educate their children; the children have the duty to support and to assist their parents. Neither the parents nor the children shall maltreat or desert one another. The foregoing provision also applies to foster parents and foster children.' [2]

The duties of parents towards their children are strictly equivalent to those of the children towards the parents, which shows that the relationship between parent and child isn't a one-sided property relationship. Parental authority is not codified in law. This legal absence of parental rights, backed up by the ever-increasing material independence of children, is no accident, nor is it a mere public show of democracy. It underlies and reinforces all ongoing struggles to ensure that political unity and consciousness become the only criteria of discipline throughout social life, *as they already are in the family*.

THE POLITICS OF CONTRACEPTION

Children are no longer the only *raison d'être* of the new Chinese woman, and nor is motherhood her sole destiny. We can evaluate the extent of women's emancipation by examining the crucial and very practical issue of contraception.

We were introduced to Li Chang, a young woman in charge of family planning in the Shawan commune. She started by explaining how the family planning centre had been set up a few years earlier at the request of a few women. At that time a doctor from the nearest hospital, accompanied by two medical workers, came to help them. Within a few days they had learnt the necessary physiology and all the basic techniques, and had begun to visit families. They encountered a variety of responses. Some women would refuse to limit their families to two or three children, especially if they had only daughters. Some husbands wouldn't accept that contraception could concern them, and only long discussion could convince them otherwise. On the other hand, sometimes a woman would immediately join the group and their work would advance by rapid strides.

'We've educated the village people about different contraceptive methods,' Li Chang continued, 'and today I think that sterilization, along with the coil and the diaphragm, are the most popular methods.' We were rather surprised and even a little shocked by this revelation, but the young woman added, 'You know, here in the village, out of a total of eighty-five sterilizations, seventy have been performed on men, because we always try very hard to make the villagers appreciate that contraception is intimately connected with the emancipation of women. A large family is still an obstacle to the woman who wants to get out of her home.'

'Don't you use the pill at all?' asked Danielle. 'We do,' replied Li Chang, 'but we're cautious about distributing it because it's still at the experimental stage. We in China try our utmost to control the long-term effects of all drugs.'

She said that abortions are performed on demand, and are almost free of charge (they cost about three yuans). The women are entitled to a fortnight's rest with full pay, as for any other medical treatment. She pointed out that childless or one-child couples were told about the risk of sterility attendant on abortion. Discussions are held with them to see if there might be a solution other than abortion for their difficulties (better housing or improved work schedules, for example). The final decision, however, rests with the couple. She also made it clear that in those rare cases where the husband opposes the abortion, it's the woman's decision alone that counts.

Li Chang explained that although the Ministry of Health has over all responsibility for family planning, every team, in the village, factory or neighbourhood, organizes its work round the specific needs of its area, thus giving the people themselves immediate control over births and the size of their families.

A visit to the maternity ward and nursery of the gynaecological hospital in Peking complemented our discussion with Li Chang. Every woman normally records the date of her periods, and these records are kept by a medical worker attached to the women's particular production unit. The records themselves provide invaluable material for medical research and the early detection of feminine ailments. Moreover pregnancy tests can be made as soon as a woman's period is overdue. Not only does this enable an early abortion to be performed under the most favourable conditions (if she wants one), it also enables the pregnancy to be medically supervised from the earliest stages. Throughout pregnancy the woman's state of health is closely watched. She may be moved right away to a less tiring job, and systematic testing may be initiated, so as to detect any potential illnesses or other dangers to the pregnancy. Such a procedure, which could well be more conscientiously carried out in the West, considerably reduces the risk of any kind of congenital malformation or handicap. Regular ante-natal consultations take place monthly until the sixth month, then twice a month until the eighth, then weekly during the eighth and ninth months.

Much the same things were felt about contraception in the Peking hospital as we had been told in Shawan: 'Contraception must not be con-

THE IDEA OF NATIONALIZATION

fused with a simple technique. It requires thorough ideological education. It is a far-reaching political act which aims to give women a method for controlling nature, so that they can participate fully in all social activities. It is a means of promoting their emancipation.'

Part Five
A CONTRIBUTION TO THE DEBATE ON SEXUALITY IN CHINA

Introduction

Extramarital sexual relations are strictly forbidden in China. No fact about China is more widely known, and in general none is less well understood. Most people are quick to see Chinese sexual *mores* as a manifestation of bourgeois puritanism or as a Stalinist bureaucratic deviation, or even as proof of the impossibility of socialism liberating women. In short, they're seen as repressive.

But the question is more complicated than such simplistic criticisms suggest.

12 Natural Needs and Cultural Needs

When it comes to revolutionary sexuality, everyone is an expert. We all know exactly what shape such sexuality will assume, and need no other yardstick by which to measure the failure of the Chinese revolution than our own preconceptions: people still marry, when marriage should have been abolished; people are rigidly monogamous, although monogamy is a sexual prison; and so on.

This sort of reasoning gets you nowhere but into the vicious circle of arguing that something is repressive because it's not free and it's free when it's not repressive. Unfortunately no one ever begins to explain what this freedom might consist of. We are reduced to mere guesswork, but even the attempt to define freedom is considered repressive.

The idea of 'natural' sexuality which supports these arguments is a very convenient one. We all have natural sexual needs and drives, so the theory goes. Different social norms suppress them and repress them in order to ensure male supremacy and to hammer submissiveness and fearful respect into us. If all such norms are eliminated, and morality itself is destroyed, sexuality will be liberated and will find its 'natural' expression. Incidentally, this subversive practice will also destroy the roots of authoritarian power in the ideological submissiveness which follows sexual repression.

This may be convenient, but unfortunately it's also completely wrong. There is no such thing as 'natural' sexuality, or else all the different forms of sexuality occurring throughout history are 'natural': it's natural that in a feudal society a man takes all the women he wants for his pleasure, his pleasure even being to take women without their consent; that in some primitive societies sexual relations take place with several partners; that in a capitalist society a woman should be a virgin when she marries, a faithful wife after her marriage to a man who is, *in fact*, polygamous before and after marriage; that in all exploiting societies battalions of women are reduced to sexual commerce, the production of pleasure for men. It's only when a ruling class collapses, dragging in its wake the morality it had forged for itself, that 'natural' sexuality is revealed for what it is: the pretence that disguises a squalid relation of exploitation.

Furthermore, not only is the allegedly natural behaviour by which we satisfy our sexual needs determined by the existing social system, but those sexual needs themselves are also the products of society. Marx said: '... production produces consumption ... by creating in the consumer a need for the objects which it first presents as products. It therefore produces the object of consumption, the mode of consumption and the urge to consume.'[1] This is no less true of sexuality.

Sexuality has become another commodity, bought and sold like the rest, subject to the laws of supply and demand like the rest, destroyed by consumption like the rest. It makes no difference whether this commodity changes hands legally or illegally, with society's blessing or without it between people of the opposite sex or of the same sex – it is still a commodity. We must ask ourselves what function our sexual culture serves in our society.

That is the fundamental question, and it must be answered before anything else.

OBJECTS OF PLEASURE AND OBJECTS OF LEISURE – PLEASURE IS FUN

Of course sex education (in which I include the lack of any formal sex education) inculcates, especially in children and women, a respect for bourgeois morality and submission to the established order. But sex education doesn't *have the monopoly* on teaching such attitudes, and that may not be the most important aspect of sex education. In a society where the division of labour becomes more accentuated, where the vast majority of people are deliberately deprived of creativity, where work has no other value than its explicit *monetary one*, sexuality becomes *a means of escaping from society through self-centered sexual consumption, rather than the full expression of interpersonal relationships*. This can only be an illusory escape in which the fugitive merely rediscovers all society's detestable features. The relationship between oppressed and oppressor, market value, selfishness, consumption for consumption's sake – are all there in another form. But illusion though it may be, it is nevertheless an important vehicle by means of which the ruling class can impose its own ethics and its vulgar materialism on the people in the guise of the true meaning of life.

'Work,' says the spokesman for bourgeois morality, 'is too often repetitive and tiring. This is, unfortunately, the hidden face of our industrial society. But while we pay a price for progress, it is a price we have to pay if progress is what we want. For production is progress and it is progress that gives everyone a television set and a car, that allows them to dress in the latest fashion, to enjoy themselves, to have some free time for leisure, that, in short, enables them to consume.' This is his morality, and he would like it to be ours. Isn't sexuality's social function to serve as a compensation for joyless work, the justification for a hopeless existence? Bourgeois sexual culture is like danger money: in exchange for ill-health, maiming or death, the workers are offered a few extra pence in their pay packets. In turning sexuality and sexual pleasure (what pleasure? pleasure for whom?) into a reward, a leisure activity, capitalism has turned it into just another aspect of wage earning. For more than one reason, the idea of sex as a 'warrior's rest' is a scandal in our sexual lives. It involves 'service' by women, who are treated as mere commodities and objects. It puts sex on *exactly* the same level as eating, drinking and sleeping. It turns sexual satisfaction into a restorative for the workforce, It reduces sex to the same level of mundane requirement as proteins, clothing, television, education and leisure activities.

Repression of sexuality and repressive sexuality

Bourgeois sexual politics, the specific lines drawn between bourgeois sexual freedoms and taboos, help to create a repressive sexual culture, partly by the prohibition of certain sexual practices, but mainly by giving sexual relations market values – by turning the relationship into a transaction between an alienated man and a subjugated woman.

The man and woman can't help reproducing their social roles within what seems to them to be their own and free domain. They carry into it the social patterns of dominant male and dominated female. Sado-masochism, passivity – aggression, potency and frigidity merely translate into sexual terms the everyday reality of oppression. Of course this doesn't mean that the woman will always be the masochistic, passive or frigid partner. Roles can always be reversed within an individual relationship, but the cultural form is perpetuated by the oppression of women and the generalized pattern of their subservience to men. A common attitude in the new women's movement is that precisely because sexuality is a taboo area for the bourgeoisie and should not be discussed, the movement must speak out. We shall criticize the prevailing morality! they proclaim. We shall leave no stone unturned! We shall prepare the ground for revolutionary attitudes! But as soon as the struggle starts, the new women's movement throws in the sponge. What have we heard from the movement since it took up this question? 'It's unfair for men to have sexual freedom when we don't.' It has proclaimed the right of women to enjoy the same freedom as men. But since when have the oppressed demanded the right to do as the oppressors do? If you understand (and therefore denounce) the repressiveness that is the outstanding feature of male sexuality, what can you hope to gain by adopting similar sexual attitudes? Basically, the bourgeoisie couldn't care less whether or not anybody talks about sexuality, but it dreads the moment when the sickening emptiness on which sexuality is founded will be exposed. To say that the bourgeoisie is repressive because it forbids the practice of sexual 'deviations' is to say exactly what the bourgeoisie wants to hear. 'Deviation' is not where the bourgeoisie says it is, but precisely where it says it is not – between the respectable sheets of the conjugal bed.

I have been using the terms 'male domination' and 'female passivity' because they refer to a facet of the reality I have been considering. But we must recognize that these two opposite aspects of our culture are simply complementary aspects of the same bourgeois sexual ideology. It isn't that bourgeois sadism on the one hand is ranged against progressive masochism on the other, just as sadism is never clearly a male attribute nor masochism a female one. There is a wide range of culturally significant forms of more or less covert sado-masochism, each one more or less confused with the others.

The bourgeoisie, like all exploiting classes, finds its pleasure in the master/slave relationship. The orgies of our rulers or marriages in the smartest churches in Paris; pornography; striptease, in Pigalle for the masses or at the Crazy Horse Saloon for company directors; prostitutes or high-class call-girls; the vice squad or the priests' confessional – all these are just variations on a single theme: the manufacture of pleasure out of intolerable oppression, at a price to suit every pocket and with an eye to all tastes.

The causes of our sexual repression do not lie in setting limitations on our behaviour, because *all* sexual behaviour has been repressed and perverted by the profound humiliation and commercialism natural to our society. *Sexual repression is integral to sexuality; it does not conflict with sexuality, it determines it.*

No one could hope to escape from this oppression merely by breaking out of the confines of legally sanctioned sexuality, because that's not what creates it. We have constant proof of this. For example there is a moral prohibition on extramarital sex for women. Whenever a married woman has sex with her husband, she acts in the socially prescribed manner – she acquiesces in and reinforces the subjugation of female to male, and her dependence on him. Whenever a woman wants to counter this repression and has sex with someone who is not her husband, she breaks the prohibition, but realizes, to her dismay, that the repression has not disappeared. Lenin, writing to Inès Armand, commented:

'Even a fleeting passion and intimacy' are 'more poetic and cleaner' than 'kisses without love' of a (vulgar and shallow) married couple. That is what you write ... Is the contrast logical? Kisses without love between a vulgar couple are *dirty*. I agree to them one should contrast ... what? One would think: kisses *with* love? While you contrast them with 'fleeting' (why fleeting?) 'passion' (why not love?) – so, logically, it turns out that kisses without love (fleeting) are contrasted with kisses without love by married people ... Strange ... Would it not be better to contrast philistine-intellectual-peasant ... vulgar and dirty marriage without love to proletarian civil marriage with love ... ? [2]

Although it's easier now to understand the way in which sexual politics are alienating, humiliating and repressive, it's still no easier to understand what precise alternatives are posed in society. If we cannot see that side of the contradiction it will be impossible for us to understand why contemporary capitalism is characterized by confused and problematic sexual mores, while the sexual mores of feudal society, for example, which were fundamentally as repressive, did not create a conflict of such magnitude.

All the evidence shows that the interest aroused by the sexual question among young people and in the new women's movement cannot simply be the idle imaginings of the unemployed petty bourgeoisie.

We have already said that the repressive nature of bourgeois sexuality is manifested more *in the type of practice it invites* than in the activities it proscribes. Bourgeois sexuality is nothing more than an exchange of commodities, surreptitiously introduced *under the guise of romantic love*. This seems to be the nub of the contradiction. The desire for a love relationship conflicts with the economic aspect of that kind of relationship, which is increasingly being revealed. Capitalism engendered this important contradiction, because only capitalism provides the material base for romantic love.

When capitalism destroyed family-based feudal production and 'liberated' the proletariat, it also made it possible for new relationships to be based on personal inclination alone. There's no law against relationships between men and women from different social classes – a working-class man can marry a middle-class woman and a cinema usherette can become a millionaire's wife. But if the only reason for embarking on a relationship with one person rather than another is the 'free choice' of those concerned, the fact that anyone embarks on such a relationship at all is always determined by external material circumstances. 'I'm getting married *to Paulette* because I love her and she loves me. But I'm getting *married* because I can't manage any other way.' So that love, being the only motive for the affair, is always contradicted by the material imperative of the affair. Loving freely and without constraint, while apparently within our reach, is always strangled by the prosaic demands of economics. There is no freedom to love, only parole – our illusions of freedom are periodically shattered by our return to the penitentiary we are occasionally allowed to think we have left behind us. All love's 'free choices' are outlined against the background of material necessity, and this necessity is the decisive criterion. Not only do we find ourselves saying, 'I know I've got to get married, but at least I can choose who I marry!', but also, 'Since I've got to have a wife who will look after my home, manage on the housekeeping money, prepare my meals, give me affection and devote herself to my happiness so that I won't be alone any more, *I shall have to try to fall in love with* a woman who will make a good, thrifty, hard-working and loving housewife.' 'Freedom' to love is expressed in the last analysis in the same terms as all capitalist 'freedoms'. It looks fine on paper, but in fact it is almost casually flouted and contradicted daily.

Sexual repression becomes intolerable because it is based on a 'freely chosen' union which generates sexual, intellectual and emotional needs, while it is in fact a contract between two partners who are not free and who seek different and antagonistic goals in this union. The man looks for a way to fill his leisure time, while the woman looks for a way to justify her confinement in the service of her family. But even the most sincere feelings and the least calculated desires can't stand up for long to the pressure of reheated stews and washing socks. The freely selected wife, the chosen one, rapidly becomes 'a nagging bitch'; the husband becomes no more than the provider; and sex is just another entry in the catalogue of disappointments which runs the gamut from the most bitter to the most harmless.

The same thing happens to love as it does to all revolutionary aspirations that emerge from the heart of capitalist society. All of them are trampled under the inexorable tread of material necessity which opposes them. *They are repressed*; they aren't yet able to realize themselves in practice; but they do exist. Revolutionary aspirations are the exact opposite of myths: they are the future society in embryo. The desire for love also tolls the knell for the old world.

Only men and women who are equally free will be able to form non-repressive and free sexual relationships. So without the emancipation of women there can be no end to sexual repression. Looking for sexual freedom without this emancipation and, even worse, seeing it as a means of achieving emancipation are more than just political traps. Such mistaken attitudes help unwittingly to strengthen a bourgeoisie which didn't even ask for help. There is no economic, political or ideological reason why the bourgeoisie couldn't eventually tolerate all the specific sexual activities that it now finds impermissible, but such licence is of no value in the struggle for liberation. The experience of the Scandinavian countries, or even of the United States, should be enough to convince anyone of that. To say otherwise is to imagine that the capitalist superstructure of bourgeois ideology, including sexual *mores*, is rigidly defined. In fact the reverse couldn't be more true. The superstructure is constantly adapting and continuously adjusting to developments at the material base. Contradictions which were latent only yesterday are nakedly revealed today. The bourgeoisie can authorize every sexual activity it wants and introduce any sexual novelty it likes, subject only to the condition that sexuality remains within the limits of its own immoral morality – an egocentric practice that is not simply divorced from the rest of society but, moreover, is a social drug of special significance. [3]

There is no returning to the 'paradise lost' of natural and free sexuality. We can't confront bourgeois sexuality with some off-the-peg revolutionary sexuality. We can only achieve revolutionary sexuality in the course of struggle against bourgeois morality and as an aspect of the transformation of all social relations between men and women. Women must undoubtedly be the architects of the new revolutionary morality, for it is they who suffer most from bourgeois sexuality and it is they who have known its most repressive moments. And that means that they must be involved in the revolutionary transformation of society.

13 A New Sexual Culture is Beginning in China

MARRIAGE – A VOLUNTARY ASSOCIATION OF EQUALS?

The first task to be tackled is quite clearly to attack everything in the old sexual *mores* which formerly extolled male supremacy. Men and women must be allowed the same sexual standards, even if these standards are only temporary. This seems to me to be the major positive feature of the new Chinese sexual morality. There is no double standard and no special allowances are made for men. The ongoing ideological struggle for late marriages and the discrediting of extramarital sexual relations concern men and women equally. And if newly married women are usually sexually inexperienced, the same is true of their husbands.

One question springs to mind. If the correct approach is to put all male-female relations on an egalitarian footing, why is it necessary to preach this kind of equality in marriage? Wouldn't it have been better to allow women the sexual freedom that men already enjoyed? Wouldn't it have been better simply to allow marriage to transform itself into a voluntary association of equals? An experiment on these lines was tried in the Soviet Union immediately after the Revolution. A series of laws were introduced to make the transformation smoother. They ensured that a couple who lived together would have the same rights and duties as a legally married couple; that divorce could be obtained at the request of either partner; and that the partners would be allowed title to their own goods in a joint estate, so that a husband could no longer seize his wife's property.

But in a society where women have *not* escaped inferior status, such judicial equality can only *reinforce* actual inequality.

Men were given a free hand to practise a new, legalized form of polygamy. They changed wives as the fancy took them, abdicating all responsibility for their children. Since peasants could not employ paid labour, they would sometimes marry in the spring to get an extra hand for the harvest, and divorce after harvest time to avoid being saddled with an extra mouth to feed during the winter months. Within record time the Soviet courts were flooded with legal actions from women who'd been deserted as soon as they'd become pregnant. [1]

The majority of women weren't wage earners and they had no economic independence at all, so that the law setting up joint estates actually worked against them. Husbands controlled all the money they earned. They were the masters and their wives would be forced to choose between submitting to a man and being deserted and left penniless. And as for the idea of love that accompanied the Soviet measures, it reduced the sexual act to no more than the satisfaction of a base appetite. Only reactionary women, full of petty-bourgeois notions, could refuse something as innocuous as drinking a glass of water. These ideas acquired the force of law and enabled men to exercise enormous ideological pressure on women in attempts to force them to relinquish their 'archaic sentimentality'. This is admirably illustrated in a survey made among *Komsomol* (Communist Youth) members at the beginning of the twenties. The question, 'Is the abolition of prostitution a problem for young men?' elicited the common reply that the young men had no need to turn to prostitutes, because 'we can have all the *Komsomol* girls we want for nothing'. This encouraged the revival of a reactionary movement among women, who, when asked the same question, would reply with a demand to reopen the brothels, which in their eyes gave them greater 'security'.

Laws exist only because there are social inequalities. Either they are meant to maintain these inequalities – bourgeois laws – or to eradicate them – revolutionary laws. What use would laws be if there was true equality for everyone? From whom or what would such laws protect us? We need unequal laws to establish equality.

Every step in Chinese legislation is guided by this view. In discussing legislation about women, the periodical *La Nouvelle Chine* emphasizes: 'Not only does Chinese law contain no discriminatory clauses against women, not only does it repeatedly proclaim the equality of the sexes, but it also adds special protective measures, *that is to say discriminating clauses against men.*' The article goes on to give specific examples:

> The Marriage Law stipulates, in article 18, that a man cannot apply for divorce while his wife is pregnant or during the year following the birth, but a pregnant woman or a woman who has just given birth is allowed to divorce. The first sentence of article 21 states that after the divorce, if the mother is given custody of a child, the father is responsible for part or the whole of the necessary cost of maintaining the child, but the law does not state that the mother is responsible for the cost of maintenance when the father is given custody. According to article 24, the husband is responsible for paying joint debts where the joint property is insufficient to cover that payment. Article 23 on the disposal of property after divorce specifies that only the wife is always allowed to retain property she owned before marriage. [2]

Incidentally, article 11 of the Marriage Law states that husband and wife have the right to keep his or her own family name and first name, and other articles ensure equal rights on similar issues.

While in the Soviet Union *de facto* marriage co-existed alongside legal marriage, China has deliberately opted for legal marriage (even though special measures are taken to ensure that children born outside marriage have the same rights and enjoy the same consideration as other children. In particular the natural father, like any divorced father, is held responsible for the maintenance of his child, and the child, like the child of any married couple, is allowed to inherit property from his natural parents.) However a closer analysis shows that marriage in China is nearer to a voluntary association of equals than the Soviet *de facto* marriage was.

It's important in this discussion to understand that both legal marriage and voluntary association have the same basic function in any given society. In a pamphlet published by the Dimitriev group of the French Women's Liberation Movement the following demands are made: 'Abolition of the institution of marriage. Recognition of voluntary association.' ³

Such 'recognition' of voluntary association can be of no value except as a means of accentuating the repressive character of the legal marriages it would mimic. It's scandalous that a man and woman who live together without legalizing their relationship should be deprived of the few rights and privileges accorded to married couples, such as legitimacy of their children, the right to Social Security benefits based on the husband's contributions, automatic rights of inheritance, and the right to a death grant and a widow's pension. It is right to demand the recognition of voluntary associations to free them from moral, social and material discrimination. But that is the only reason why such a demand should be made. For if the institution of marriage is abolished and voluntary association is recognized, doesn't the latter simply become marriage by another name? (In any case, voluntary associations, particularly among the working class, have in fact been just that for a long time. 'Setting up home' is one of the ways of being 'a family' and involves the same tasks and the same constraints as the legally recognized equivalent.) The Dimitriev group has put forward a laughable idea – the family structure itself is no longer the source of repression, selfishness and submissiveness; the source is now held to be the marriage contract instead. Get rid of the marriage service and release woman from her servitude!

THE TWO PRINCIPAL SCANDALS OF BOURGEOIS MARRIAGE

In capitalist societies, marriage is reactionary for two reasons. The first is the wife's economic dependence on her husband, which entails her being seen as inferior – this inferior status may or may not be codified in law, in the familiar terms, for example, of 'to love, honour and obey'. The second is the legal indissolubility of the marriage bond, or at least the extreme difficulty of breaking it. Emphasizing a formal solution in voluntary association involves a preoccupation with this second aspect of oppression in marriage. But if women (including some who aren't legally married), abandon the idea of regaining their freedom even when they're bitterly unhappy, they do so because the main obstacle to their freedom is the economic

impossibility of supporting themselves and their children.
Thus economic independence for the woman is the first condition of any truly voluntary association. Without it the prescriptions for voluntary associations, or communes, or free love to transform relations between the sexes are no more effective than bandages round a wooden leg.

The material independence of women is an absolutely necessary precondition for voluntary associations to work, but it isn't, by any means, sufficient. Furthermore, no simple legal demand will alter the fact that the marriage bond is, in the main, considered to be indissoluble. Such a demand has to be backed up by a revolution in male ideas about the value of women. The complete freedom to break up a union must not simply enable men to *continue* to use women as disposable objects. There's no reason to hope that the legalization of this age-old male custom could effect *in the slightest* the desired transformation in male–female relations. The freedom to change partners, previously the undeclared prerogative of men, must aim to revalue the reasons why two people live together if it is actually to be progressive. When two people are no longer held together by material constraints they usually stay together because they love one another. Material freedom allows love to realize its full potential, but bourgeois society involves so many imperatives forcing people to stay together that love becomes redundant, at most a pretext for staying together.

Voluntary associations can represent real progress only if they are accompanied by sexual equality, the destruction of the economic function of the family and the transformation of relations between adults and children.

Words are not enough! Unless these conditions actually exist, the only freedoms represented by voluntary association are the freedom of men to oppress women and the freedom of parents to oppress their children – the same freedoms that the bourgeois institution of marriage offers today.

Freedom of choice

I could say that Chinese marriage, despite appearances, is approaching true voluntary association precisely because the Chinese revolution explicitly aims to realize the necessary conditions for voluntary associations to work. There is one other fact which indicates that China proposes voluntary association *in practice* if not in so many words. It is the fact that the Chinese have freedom of choice in selecting their spouses.

Two people in our society get together only after considering all sorts of practicalities and after making all manner of calculations. The calculations of the bourgeois are well known – they count the dowry, consider the inheritance and weigh the wife's new social life against her lost opportunities before making any decisions. It often begins to look as though the marriage has been prearranged. No demands are made on the woman except to provide heirs and to behave as befits a lady – but that's a categorical imperative. As for the husband, who will have the privilege of initiating his 'innocent' wife into the sorry duties of the conjugal bed, he will already have found compensations elsewhere and is secure in the knowledge that he will be able to go on enjoying them outside the marriage.

However, the bourgeoisie doesn't have a monopoly on calculating the 'interest' or otherwise of a marriage. The other social classes also indulge in this practice, although their criteria are less degenerate. The peasant who has no alternative but to till his land will also look for a wife who displays the required qualities for her future tasks. She will be sturdy, hard-working and have a life-long familiarity with peasant life. A shorthand-typist doesn't easily exchange her notebook for a pitch fork. The young working-class girl also calculates her chances of getting a man with a secure job, a car and a home before she stumbles not-so-blindly into love. As for practicality, we have only to look at the many thousands of unromatic marriages to see that 'freedom of choice' is a phrase as empty as 'love at first sight'. One woman marries her next-door neighbour, because he's the first man who's proposed to her. Another marries the father of her child, because our society forces her to. These women marry so as not to be alone, because alone they are outcasts and economically at a disadvantage. Do any of these women – and they represent most women in our society – exercise freedom of choice? If you are going to talk of the voluntary association of equals, you must at least recognize the need to create the conditions on which true freedom of choice depends. This is not simply a matter of banning arranged or other compulsory marriages. Men and women alike must achieve genuine control over their own lives – a control which need never yield to any economic or ideological constraints, which is exercised with complete awareness. This can be achieved only by following objective political criteria, in line with the present, diversified social practice determining the framework within which the choice of sexual partner is made.

What material conditions is China currently trying to develop so that true voluntary associations of equals will be possible? The answer to this question will judge the truth of the matter.

LATE MARRIAGE

While the Chinese are allowed to marry from the age of eighteen, an extensive campaign is being waged throughout the country to urge the young not to get married until they are in their late twenties. The importance of this issue was stressed everywhere we went on our visit. But the explanations we were given for it weren't always very convincing. For example we were often told, sometimes by officials, that late marriage was a way to keep the birthrate down. But to say that is to ignore the *main* aim of family planning: the advancement of women's emancipation.

Family planning in China is explicitly linked to women's liberation, as Han Suyin confirms; 'Voluntary motherhood must be founded on the *emancipation of the woman*, on her equality, her right to study and to participate in all political decision-making, as well as on her increased social awareness. The political and economic emancipation of women has been

A NEW SEXUAL CULTURE IS BEGINNING IN CHINA 149

the first condition for the success of any mass family-planning campaign.' [4]

We must also realize that abstinence as a *'contraceptive' method* is a bit rudimentary. Which makes it difficult to understand how the one and only goal of reducing the birthrate could justify delaying marriages. The same extensive propaganda campaign could just as easily be used to encourage the young to use other contraceptive methods and to put off having a child until their late twenties. There is no reason to believe that the masses of young people who have voluntarily put off getting married couldn't have married when they wished and refrained from reproducing themselves by methods other than abstinence.

But despite these objections, late marriage in China remains a revolutionary measure of great importance, for altogether different reasons. These reasons are worth considering.

I have repeatedly said that equality between the sexes is never complete during the socialist period. Without any doubt, late marriage is a means of promoting equality which takes account of this inequality. It's easy to understand that a woman of twenty-six who has worked and been self-sufficient, who has taken part in various cultural activities and youth work, who has shouldered political and social responsibilities, who has spent a year or more in a people's commune, who has been a member of the people's militia, who has then gone on to university or various study schools, who has made many friends from many different walks of life and who has, in short, broadened her outlook on society, will have carved out for herself a firm foothold from which to resist any future pressure from husband or society to 'keep to her kitchen'. The economic, political and ideological independence gained over a period of ten or so years is a powerful motive force for wives and mothers to continue the active struggle for their emancipation. The fact that Chinese women don't throw themselves blindly into marriage, that they don't escape their parents' nest just to start their own, is refreshing, but even more, it's enviable. If this were all, it would be enough to show that late marriage is a revolutionary measure. But there's even more to it than that.

14 A New Idea of Love

The wide-ranging knowledge and practical experience of Chinese youth have given them a new perspective on love and the family. That's not to say that they have rejected love as a futile gesture, but that they can now struggle against idealism in love from the position of strength of materialism. Oppressed women are particularly prone to this idealist disease. For them love becomes the bearer of all hopes and all disappointments – the extent of its idealization is in direct ratio to their lack of social experience, to their being cut off from other social activities. As a consequence, every interaction with their husband is distorted, as is every judgement about reality.

The proper perspective on love doesn't devalue it. On the contrary, love seen in context is revalued in the light of its practice. If love entails withdrawal from society, the abandonment of the revolution and complete devotion to one's partner, then it will be rejected, for it can only be damaging. But if you see love in its context, relative to all other aspects of social life, you see it as part of everything else you already wish to do. The special relationship you have with this man must help you and him to reach a complete and conscious fulfilment of your social roles.

The advantage of prolonged celibacy as it is practised in China is to avoid the privatization of love and to give it back its context in a revolutionary society. The warmth and affection the Chinese couple give to one another arise naturally out of their devotion to the people and the warmth they give to all their comrades. The progressive transformation of the work situation, which we have already discussed, means that both partners can expect the other to be politically committed to his or her work. Since the family is no longer the centre of interest, each partner is expected to be involved in a variety of areas. Since relationships between parents and children are no longer run on authoritarian and self-centred lines, each partner is expected to have a responsible and fraternal attitude towards the children. Of course the social experience of the young is an enormous stimulus to the growth of practical knowledge about one another – knowledge which can be used to gauge objectively the different qualities people require of their partners. There can be no doubt at all that late

A NEW IDEA OF LOVE

marriage can contribute only as much to the revolution as that experience will allow. Without such experience, late marriage would be worse than useless.

How could a convent girl of the nineteenth century, unmarried at twenty-five, have learnt anything that would motivate her own emancipation? How could a son of the bourgeoisie, advised to remain a bachelor until his late twenties, bring to his late marriage anything but the corrupt morality of his parents? She would have spent a vital period cloistered with nuns. He will spend it in a highly lucrative job or as an officer doing military service in an imperialist army, ensuring his future marital bliss by bedding any and every girl he can, learning through the exercise of this 'inalienable right' that women are no better than the contemptible objects of his own juvenile pleasure. In our society it would actually be progressive for such a young man to break with tradition and marry, at eighteen, the young student he so 'innocently' loves.

In her commentary on the Marriage Law, Teng Ying-chao writes: 'Nevertheless we oppose the idea that 'love is supreme' just as much as we oppose those who trifle with love. Besides, we are opposed to those things which are insufficient to guarantee a lasting love, such as social status, money, appearance, etc., as conditions of love and marriage.' [1]

There is a story about a young Chinese student leader during the Cultural Revolution. He was filled with the spirit and fire of revolution and was worshipped by a whole group of women students. One day some of the women got together to talk about why the comrade had so many women admirers. 'Several of you are in love with this comrade,' said one of the women. 'I've been told that you love him for his revolutionary qualities, but I'm not convinced of that. I think there's another reason which I'd like you to consider carefully. Because of his qualities this comrade has great prestige among the intellectuals. We have given him important responsibilities. He is listened to. Those who are troubled or confused willingly go to see him, to talk to him and to ask for his advice and help. This is only natural. But, I ask you, isn't it precisely because he is such a luminary that he is "loved" by so many girls? Isn't it really his leadership that they love? That's what I feel. And that's why I think there's something bourgeois about this infatuation. It seems to me that our comrade students are copying a bourgeois male–female relationship.'

This story illustrates the meaning of class love better than I could. It is not enough simply to state that you couldn't *love* a counter-revolutionary to destroy the class aspect of love and to transform it. You must also make sure that love is no longer full of bourgeois attitudes.

Good looks don't escape the class struggle

As Teng advocated, and as should by now be obvious, a person's looks are irrelevant to marriage. But how does the bourgeois image of beauty reveal its class nature, so that the canon of good looks can be discarded? In class society female beauty is always the prerogative of the ruling class. It decrees, for the whole of society, what a beautiful woman should look like. To be beautiful in the West is to look like a bourgeois woman, an indolent lady of means whose status is announced by her attitude and gestures, her clothes and hairstyle. And this is no natural beauty (if such a thing exists), but a confection of purchasable ingredients − a pinch of hairdressing, a dash of *couture* and a spoonful of low-calorie food all garnished with a sprinkling of make-up and a heavy dose of plastic surgery. The world of women's magazines is a hymn to this type of beauty. In 'my lady's' account books you can usually find one column for the 'beauty budget'. The ostentatious luxury of such beauty reflects not only the power and prestige of money in our society but also, and most significantly, the role of sex object that has fallen to women. All this is almost brazenly translated in the advertiser's image of women, in which 'a woman's face and figure are her fortune'.

Beauty like this is beyond the reach of most women, not just *financially* but also because of the lifestyle it entails. Even when she's dolled up the woman who works in the fields or on an assembly line won't be able to hide her calloused hands and her arms and body, which have become muscular with work. The housewife who spends her life washing clothes, ironing, cooking, cleaning windows won't be able to cover the marks of physical or nervous exhaustion with make-up, and no finery will disguise her weariness when evening comes. And yet the man she lives with, just like all the others, is conditioned to desire the very type of beauty which she can't afford − and that too is a significant facet of sexual repression.

This image of woman no longer exists in China. You will be greeted by a completely different image there − on wall posters, in newspapers, on the stage, everywhere. It is the picture of a worker or a peasant, with a determined expression and dressed very simply. She is always shown doing one of the daily tasks that the millions of Chinese women know from experience. You can see her working, studying, taking part in a demonstration or simply laughing, but you will never see her in any of the unreal and mystifying situations and stances that the advertising image-makers construct for us. This transformation of the female image reveals the new place of women in society, and undoubtedly also serves to focus men's attention on to the changes that are necessary in their relationships with women.

Contemporary Chinese theatre is concerned both to criticize the idea of love as a refuge and to advance the practice of the new love. This is particularly striking in *The White-haired Girl*. The co-author who revised it at the time of the Cultural Revolution discussed the play with us in great detail during our stay in Shanghai.

He told us that the kind of love that was depicted in the first version of the play had been the subject of bitter controversy. The two main protagonists are Hsi-erh − the white-haired girl − who is a poor peasant and an ardent revolutionary, and her fiancé, Ta-chun, who is also a poor peasant and a soldier in the PLA. The two meet again after the Japanese invaders have been driven from their village, and in the original ending, marry and live happily ever after. Some people approved of this ending and tried desperately hard to keep it, arguing that it was normal and right and proper that the couple should think of themselves once they had struggled against the Japanese and finally won. The revolutionaries, on the other hand, condemned the ending as sentimental and wanted it to be radically rewritten. Eventually the revolutionaries won this particular artistic battle and a new ending was written. In this version the victory over the Japanese leads to Hsi-erh and Ta-chun deciding to continue the struggle, but this time against Kuomintang troops. Now the play stresses that no one can 'live happily ever after' while his or her country is being put to fire and sword. A love born out of common hatred against oppression cannot grow freely under the yoke of that oppression, be it domestic, colonial or imperialist. This idea of love closely linked to social reality is diametrically opposed to the bourgeois idealistic conception of love. There is nothing mystical or magical in Hsi-ehr's and Ta-chun's love, there is no magnetic attraction and no love at first sight. But there is an identical background of suffering, a shared anger and a common will to struggle. They love one another because they share the same hatred of the old society and the same determination to create a new one. In her refusal to conform to the traditional stereotype of the seduced, fragile and submissive woman, Hsi-ehr loves Ta-chun as an equal. He doesn't protect her – they help one another. We don't have to choose between love or struggle, but only between *the ways in which we will love one another*. We can do it selfishly, escaping from reality, or we can do it by living in the real world and struggling to change it. Love can then become encouragement and mutual support in that struggle. Hsi-ehr's feelings are not incompatible with her revolutionary commitment; they are an expression of it.

WE MUST NOT CONCLUDE ...

It would be an obvious mistake to conclude from all that has gone before that love and sexuality no longer present problems in China. For one thing, how could any society produce a perfectly satisfactory or even an exemplary sexual culture when its women aren't yet fully liberated? As Mao Tse-tung has said, '*Every kind of thinking, without exception, is stamped with the brand of class.*' What miracle could allow sexuality to escape this rule? For example it's clear that strictly demographic interpretations of late marriage can only diminish its revolutionary scope. But on the other hand it's one manifestation of the class struggle that all things are open to a variety of interpretations, and such diversity is unavoidable.

It seems to me that revolutionaries often make the mistake of not criticizing right-wing interpretations firmly enough, so that 'peaceful co-existence' appears to be the watchword in what should be the arena of ideological struggle. Naturally this absence of polemic can only have negative results in practice. Take the case of late marriage that I discussed above. The failure to criticize the overt rationale given for late marriage has resulted in many Chinese people accepting it and adhering to strict monogamy not because of their revolutionary convictions but out of moral conformity – which is not the desired state of affairs.

The revolution and the people – men and women – who make it have nothing to fear from an open ideological struggle about love and sexuality. Why aren't the Chinese waging this struggle? Some Chinese comrades themselves attempted to give us an answer. 'Sexual education,' they said, 'is difficult, because even our political cadres have an inadequate political and ideological grounding in the subject, because the people are reticent, because the myth of virility is still strong, because the old mentality which sees this area as shameful still survives . . .' All the more reason, surely, to open the debate! There can be little worry that love and sexuality will become central preoccupations to the exclusion of other, more immediate, concerns. Chinese society manages to conduct many debates without any of them becoming popular and political obsessions.

In spite of these criticisms, the Chinese policy on love and sexuality is *in no way* comparable to conventional Judeo-Christian morality. *This is another case where separating some social phenomenon from the new social relations underlying it results in a failure to understand anything at all about it.* And judging policies on the basis of ostensible ideological explanations alone is less satisfactory in this area than in any other. For such judgements will always be misguided if they ignore the practical results of political decisions. With love and sexuality, for example, we must look at the effects of Chinese policy on the emancipation of women.

A society cannot conceal the evidence of its treatment of women as sex objects, and China shows no such evidence. I don't doubt that the new sexual attitudes held by Chinese youth, judged by some to be too severe, have actually had an enormous influence in helping Chinese women to shake off their former status. Furthermore, if sexuality and love are closely bound up together – as they are in China – sexuality will be altogether more valued and more valuable – as it is in China. To lose sight of these things would prevent us from making any judgement with a materialist basis.

We can have some idea, albeit embryonic, of what love, sexual morality and the family will be like in the future by taking what exists today as a starting-point. But the Chinese experience has taught us that there is no 'natural' or 'innate' revolutionary morality which is simply waiting to be applied to concrete situations. A new and revolutionary sexual morality and a proletarian viewpoint in sexuality, love and the family can only be gradually constructed (and not necessarily in a linear fashion) through the practice of the class struggle, and within the revolutionary movement against the ancient traditions, divisions and reactionary functions that have enslaved women.

In Place of a Conclusion

The road to women's liberation via the Chinese revolution has been only roughly sketched. To see it in greater detail requires a clear understanding of Chinese society, its past history as well as its present contradictions – an understanding, clearly, that we have yet to achieve.

We also need to understand more about all manifestations of women's oppression in our own countries. Such understanding comes only with an unlimited awareness and ever closer contact with the mass of our women compatriots. To the question, 'What is to be done?', the only proper answer is, 'Everything!'

The women of today are involved in their own struggle because in the past their oppression has always been denied, and their revolutionary hopes and dreams have always been reduced to a slim catalogue of legislative and budgetary demands appended to the end of any self-respecting party manifesto. And yet that struggle will not be understood, and therefore will not succeed, as long as we in the women's movement ignore the other forms of exploitation suffered by other oppressed people. Some members of the Women's Liberation Movement have attacked this idea in the mistaken belief that it would be mere charity. But to pay heed to others' oppression doesn't mean acting 'charitably' to those who are oppressed. Rather it means understanding that women's oppression is like all oppression – the product of an exploiting society, in our case a capitalist society. It means that the only way women have of achieving their liberation is via the revolution.

Whether we like it or not, women as a group and the proletariat are interdependent – not like two playing cards which support one another, nor like two nations allied together, but in the same way as the links of a chain *are interdependent*. If criticism of female roles and functions is our starting-point, and if our aim is truly to expose the real link link between the specific oppression of women and the entire social edifice of exploitation, then we must raise our sights to a global critique of society.

Seen in such a light this book stands as a contribution to the vital debate on the role of women in our revolution – a debate that is only just beginning.

Appendix: Some Statistics on the Participation of Women in Administration (1971 figures)

In general it is Party policy that a minimum of 30 per cent of women should work in administrative departments. For example we were told that 30 per cent of the national minorities organizers were women. In practice, whenever an administrative post falls vacant a woman will be chosen in preference to a man with equal political qualifications, if no man is found with higher qualifications.

The factory at Chao Yan

	total	women	men
workers	360	288 (80%)	72 (20%)
party cell	9	8	1
revolutionary committee	8	6	2
teams (5 teams of four members each)	20	16 (80%)	4 (20%)

It's useful to compare the ratios of men in positions of administrative responsibility to the total number of men, and of women in positions of administrative responsibility to the total number of women.

	total	women	men
inhabitants	360	288	72
party cell	9	8 (2.7%*)	1 (1.4%)
revolutionary committee	8	6 (2.1%)	2 (2.9%)
teams	20	16 (5.5%)	4 (5.5%)

* percentages of total male and female populations respectively.

The Gynaecological Hospital in Peking

	total	women	men
workers	442	420 (95%)	22 (5%)
party cell	9	5 (55%)	4 (45%)
revolutionary committee	24	10 (40%)	14 (60%)
teams (12 teams of 8 members each)	96	77 (80%)	19 (20%)

Because of the surplus of women in the hospital as a whole, the above figures are not as significant as the figures given in the table below, which shows percentages of the total make and female populations:

	women	men
party cell	5 (1.2%)	4 (19%)
revolutionary committee	10 (2.4%)	14 (64%)
teams	77 (18%)	19 (86%)

Since membership of party cell, revolutionary committee and team overlaps (in fact all cell and committee members are also team members) there are only 77 individual women and 19 individual men altogether in administrative positions. While the degree of participation of women usually decreases the higher you go up the leadership ladder, in this case the gap between men and women is narrower at the higher level of party cell than it is in the revolutionary committee. It may be that, given the small total of men, their participation has been artificially increased by a policy of sending male party cadres to this hospital.

The People's Commune at Shawan (near Hangchow)

	total	women/girls	men/boys
inhabitants	22,926	11,296	11,630
labour force	12,252	5820 (47.5%)	6432 (52.5%)
party committee members	110	49 (45%)	61 (55%)
'the vanguard' (elected for a term of one year)	300	287	13
youth league	422	280 (66%)	142 (34%)
women's committee members	5500	5500	–
revolutionary committee	260+	44 (16%+)	216 (84%)
permanent office of the revolutionary committee	5	2*	3

* including the vice-president

The Sino-Albanian People's Commune

	total	women/girls	men/boys
labour force	10,400	5300 (51%)	5100 (49%)
party		35%	65%
revolutionary committee		25%	75%
team officers		50%	50%

The Children's Palace in Shanghai

	total	girls	boys
full-time members	200	100	100
revolutionary committee		45%	55%
brigade members (in 4 brigades)		50%	50%
League of Red Guards	20	65%	35%

Afterword: Against the Eternal Woman[1]

'Confucius has been dead for more than two thousand years, but his rotten ideology, according to which men are lords and women their subjects is still influencing people and constantly shows itself.'

Here is an example of what can be read daily in the Chinese press. It is hardly surprising to see public recognition of the fact that ideas and doctrines against women still exist in today's China – that has been known for a long while. What is striking about these articles, and they are particularly common, is their tone, which doesn't shy away from the blunt truth, and the fact that they confirm the idea that much remains to be done before sexual equality is reached.

This stands in strong contrast to the rightist tendency that was becoming blatantly obvious until recently. This tendency held that men and women were already completely equal in China. It even led some people to come round to the view that there was no need to revive the inactive women's organization, because sexual equality was an established fact – no oppression, no problem.

This trend, fundamentally aiming to deny the class struggle and *therefore the need to struggle*, could have had grave consequences because it arises from the mistaken ideas of the people. In fact it sometimes did.

Apparently paradoxically, the rightist tendency coexisted peacefully with what could be called classic and universal anti-feminism – the sort of anti-feminism that consists of plainly and openly preaching contempt for women, on the grounds of alleged 'biological' and natural inferiority. These two trends in anti-female thought clearly differed in their terms and arguments, but both agreed on the central point: that women's initiative was to be blocked so that women would be prevented from following the recommendation printed in the *People's Daily* [2] editorial of 8 March 1973, 'to get down to action'.

This reactionary offensive is not confined to women but has the restoration of the old social order as its primary objective, and demands the relegation of women to their former inferior status as an inevitable consequence. It has met with a revolutionary counter-offensive, begun in early 1972. At that point, a few months after the death of Lin Piao, you could find calls in the press for more concern over the women's question. The 8 March editorial in the *People's Daily* gave a real boost to the grassroots revival of the Women's Liberation Movement. This revival was marked a few months later by the regional reconstruction of the Women's Federation, and the campaign has broadened as it has continued. The launching of the 'Pi Lin Pi Kong' [3] campaign at the beginning of 1973 called for massive participation by women, as we shall see.

By drawing up a provisional balance-sheet of this campaign, we can see clearly enough the areas in which the bourgeoisie has been trying hardest to effect its restoration, and how the revolutionary counter-offensive has been put into practice. At a time when women in the West are daily becoming more aware of their oppression and are joining the fight in greater and greater numbers, this new wave of the Women's Liberation Movement in China must be of interest to us.

Must women be liberated from housework?

To claim that men and women are already equal is to prevent the necessary practical steps being taken for the achievement by women of true equality. Those who express the arrogant and age-old contempt for housework find that completely to their taste. The development of domestic-service workshops, which are *material measures* of very great political significance for the liberation of women from domestic tasks, has been slowed down and sometimes even halted altogether, on the pretext that men and women are now sharing housework equally.

This pernicious tendency is doubly mistaken. Firstly, because it treats the avant-garde (although fairly widespread) practice of housework-sharing as though it was universal. Secondly, and most importantly, because the disappearance of women's work (that is domestic work) results mainly from the socialization and mechanization of specific household tasks, and not from a new egalitarian distribution of tasks between husband and wife, though such a distribution is still necessary for several reasons (see Part Two). The importance of this question is stressed in a *Red Flag* article called 'Make energetic efforts to train women cadres'.

With regard to the question of family complications of women, we must also conduct concrete analyses. In the old society, women were downgraded into 'slaves in their families'. For several thousand years the basic guiding thought of the feudal landlord and bourgeois classes was to take women as slaves and appendages, to put them in the kitchen, to tie them up with heavy household chores, and to deprive them of the right to participate in social production and political activities. *One of the important tasks of the proletariat is to liberate women from this slavery.* After liberation, the establishment of the socialist system and the participation in productive labour by the masses of women have brought fundamental changes in this situation. *However, due to the influence of the idea of the exploiting classes of looking down on women and the restrictions of the material conditions,* the question of heavy household chores has not been completely solved. [4] In fact it was not just for the reasons expressed here that domestic tasks were overlooked in the revolutionary process. I have been able to discover others in the course of recent visits. For example the contempt in which any and every form of housework was held, although vigorously denounced today, obviously slowed down the socialization of housework. Some of the then current ideas are also revealing. For example: 'Working in a service workshop is not serving the people, it's serving the private interests of the people.' Or, 'The only productive work is factory work, and only productive work is noble', which was a fairly widespread attitude among young people at a certain date. [5] Then again there was the other side of this coin in the old Liuist demagogy: 'It's *also* a revolutionary task to look after your household and your children.' [6]

But the service workshops are only the beginning of the abolition of housework. Once the domestic tasks have been taken out of family hands and collectivized they still have to be mechanized. This mechanization has its roots in two separate areas. Firstly, it clearly depends on the basic improvements effected by service workers themselves. Secondly, it depends on the development of light industry in the relevant fields. One instance where the two areas have borne fruit is in the development of collective automatic laundries. In the same way, if the actual domestic needs of the masses are not sufficiently systematized and recognized by the industrial sector, it may be difficult to appreciate that producing this or that object could be important for the liberation of women. The Women's Federation has a vital part to play in all this – organizing the mass of women, researching and pointing to their needs, acting as a pressure group to push for change. The present 'restrictions of the material conditions' referred to in the *Red Flag* article will have to be broken down. And to this end political and ideological mobilization is essential.

Training women cadres

This topic is especially interesting because it allows us to see the extent to which two allegedly opposed ideas, 'men and women are perfectly equal' and 'women are inferior to men', actually meet and coexist in perfect harmony.

The *Red Flag* article I have already cited makes it very explicit that,
... the growth of women cadres still fails to keep pace with the objective requirements of China's socialist revolution and socialist construction. In some localities the number of women party members is much too low compared with the number of revolutionary women, and there are too few women cadres in leading bodies. This unavoidably affects the development of the movement for the emancipation of women. *One who fails to see this cannot see clearly the great significance of training and bringing up women cadres and developing party membership among women, to say nothing of taking the necessary measures to solve the relevant problems.*

AFTERWORD 161

How could measures be taken which specifically encourage the training of women cadres when people happily reiterate that women already have equal rights with men in whatever sphere you care to mention?

The people who say that will rationalize the fact that there is a relatively small number of women cadres, will fail to take the necessary steps and will even excuse themselves on the grounds that women are naturally backward.

To record or to reform

As a result, such people can do no more than regret that the cultural and political level of women happens to be too low, that women happen to have too little time because of their household duties and that, unfortunately, they can't be given any responsibilities until circumstances permit. *Red Flag* takes up this point:

> Some of the comrades . . . believe that women possess 'low cultural standards and ability', that they have 'family complications', and that 'it is difficult to promote women cadres'. This kind of thinking greatly affects the growth of women cadres . . . The idea that women are less able than men is not justified by actual conditions in China . . . As for saying that the cultural standard and work ability of some women comrades are not high enough, it also has deep class origins and social historical origins. It is exactly because of this that we must show *concern* for them, train them, and help them improve themselves. We must never discriminate against them.

To say that women 'have family complications' is, to all appearances, a neutral and objective statement. To conclude from it that they can't be entrusted with responsibility is definitely a reactionary attitude, and one that the Party and the women's committees vehemently criticize. That there must be more concern for the actual and particular problems of women has been a constant theme of Chinese propaganda since the 8 March editorial. Of course performing household tasks still conflicts with the political, ideological and cultural tasks that women must assume. Denial, as we have seen, serves no purpose for women, but to be content with merely recording the conflict is not much of an advance either. Progress depends on the energetic implementation of a series of reforms which have already shown their value in many vanguard areas. [8]

That's why *Red Flag* reaffirms this necessary political stance:

> . . . it is most essential . . . to solve the contradictions between revolutionary work and family work. It is necessary to promote the practice that men and women must share household chores. At the same time, it is necessary to pay attention to the specific characteristics of women and help them solve specific problems. Late marriage and planned parenthood should be promoted. It is essential to do a good job in running social public welfare facilities, [9] such as health insurance for woman and children and nurseries. [10] So long as we adopt the correct

attitude and a number of practical measures, it is not difficult to solve the specific difficulties of women.

Only a firm and systematic application of such reforms will resolve the contradictions. By the same token, there is only one objective criterion in contemporary China by which to judge whether a policy is revolutionary or not. It need involve no theoretical consideration of the 'feminist cause', for it is simply whether or not the policy brings about reforms.

For a long time to come the training of women cadres will remain a key battleground in the struggle between revolution and counter-revolution. To have women in positions of leadership goes right against the old reactionary morality. 'If women succeed in these tasks, then what use will men be?' writes a working-class woman, making a point that had been worrying some of the husbands. Some men, those who are not really convinced of the need for equality, feel self-satisfied and happy in the belief that they have accomplished a praiseworthy feat as soon as their organizational team is increased by a few women. The article in *Red Flag* retorts:

> To select and promote women cadres and assign them to the leading bodies at various levels is only the beginning of our efforts to train and educate them and not the end of the work. To enable them to remain vigorous and keep their revolutionary spirit, we must do a lot of arduous and meticulous work. As a matter of fact, organizationally it is often relatively easy to select and appoint women cadres, but it is no easy task to help them really mature. The leadership at all levels must, therefore, attach importance to carrying out education in ideology and political line in training women cadres. It is necessary to encourage them to make progress and help them overcome their shortcomings and take up their responsibility with courage ... The essential step in training women cadres is to let them participate in the three great revolutionary movements and temper themselves in the struggles so as to raise their consciousness and work ability ... The party committees at all levels should create favourable conditions for them so as to enable them to learn more from their work and improve themselves through training ... It is necessary to place confidence in them when we employ women cadres. It is also necessary to give them adequate support in critical times and actively help them to solve their difficulties ... To train women cadres is the task of the whole Party, and it cannot be considered to be work of only certain departments ... Party committees at all levels should raise their understanding of this question to the level of the struggle between the two lines and of consolidating the dictatorship of the proletariat ... While adhering to the principle of studying on the jobs, it is necessary to carry out for them education on theory in a planned way by holding study classes, and sending them to '7 May' cadre schools ... The broad masses of women cadres should also fully understand their honourable duties in the socialist revolution and construction, acquire the determination to fulfil their tasks, dare to practise and study assiduously so as to mature rapidly, and contribute their

share in striving for still greater victories in socialist revolution and construction. Production units throughout China have sent reports to the national press about the changes brought about by following this policy and rectifying their style of work. A people's commune in Kiangsu [11] told how all its work team leaders had been men, although twelve of the teams were composed mainly of women. This had led to bad feeling. The men would treat the women's problems lightly or even completely ignore them. The women, still in the grip of age-old tradition, didn't have the courage to air their own points of view, their differences and their difficulties. During the movement of criticism against Lin Piao and the rectification of styles of work, 'the brigade conscientiously studied this problem'. New team leaders, all women, were elected. The results soon began to show. Leaders and led are more closely united; it's now possible to investigate and solve concrete problems as they occur; and the teams have made great advances in their political studies. Productivity and output have both increased by leaps and bounds. From being shy at the outset, these women have steeled themselves to their new responsibilities. Their victory has revalued the status of all other women. The lesson is clear: those who believe that nature or destiny have created women to be docile and obedient and second-rate workers are, consciously or unconsciously, taking the road of counter-revolution.

Reconstructing the women's federation

The campaign to put the women's question back into the centre of the political arena is the context in which Chinese women have entered the movement of criticism against Confucius and Lin Piao. But another influence has been of great positive value to women in the current struggle — the reconstruction of the Women's Federation. Grass-roots committees of the Women's Federation were revived all over China, and immediately became very active. Since June 1973 Women's Federation conferences have been held throughout the country.

There had been no formal organization for the majority of women since 1966. The Federation's lengthy absence can perhaps be attributed to the 'egalitarian' tendency mentioned above. Other traditional organizations were also quiescent for some years, but such inactivity must have been more harmful to women than it was to other sectors of the population. While the Youth League, the unions and the Women's Federation were all temporarily suspended, young people and workers had their own revolutionary organizations, which were necessary to that phase of the struggle which started with the great proletarian Cultural Revolution. In the Red Guard organizations, among the revolutionary rebels in the factories and later in factory conferences, young people and workers could put forward their problems and discuss them. However, women didn't usually have their own political meeting-place where they could work out together their criticisms of what was still oppressing them.

Because they suffer a specific form of oppression, women need specific organizations which will help them to participate fully in the total movement of the revolution, just as they will help the revolution to grasp the importance of any movement of half the people. [12]

Women were a motive force in the movement of criticism levelled against Confucius and Lin Pao

The reactionary ideology of the four Confucian contempts has become a common talking-point since the beginning of the campaign of criticism levelled against Confucius and Lin Piao, which has comparatively recently become nationwide. The contempts are these: for manual work, for women, for the young and for those who are governed.

It's a safe bet that the new campaign will put the women's question in the forefront of the class struggle even more forcefully than the Cultural Revolution did.

The women who wrote the following words in the *People's Daily* hit the nail on the head: 'We working women suffered most from the doctrine of Confucius . . ., so we have the greatest right to speak out in the struggle to criticise Lin Piao and Confucius.' [13]

The committees of the Women's Federation have gone to war against Confucius. Through study and otherwise, Chinese women have started to settle their accounts with an ideology that is over two thousand years old. This was so widespread and deep-rooted that you could have taken it for 'common sense'; it held on for as long as it was appropriate to the material base of the old Chinese society; but it still maintains a hold in China, even after obvious and *fundamental* social change. Confucian ideas are deeply ingrained in Chinese culture, in Chinese thought and in the Chinese people. Moreover there still exist material vestiges of the old society which continue to support the existence of these old ideas.

To put this criticism into practice will inevitably lead to a *reform of all existing archaic social relations*. And to mount the offensive it is imperative to mobilize the masses, men and women alike, for the criticism of old customs and the promotion of new socialist *mores* – even while relying on the *revolutionary relations of production that are already established*. Women must be given the chance to 'free their minds' and, step by step, to overthrow the 'eternal woman'.

The women of the Yuan Ping Street Federation, in Fukien, have written:

> During the mobilization of the women in the district to criticize Confucius, we worked out 'the five destructions and the five reconstructions', taking into account current expressions of the class struggle on the ideological level. [15]
>
>   1 To destroy feudal superstititions and to establish the thesis that work creates the world
>   2 To abolish the old matrimonial system of arbitrary (or 'forced') marriages arranged as a business transaction by parents on their

children's behalf, and to strengthen the freedom of choice in marriage that is now exercised in a new form

3 To eliminate the ideology of male supremacy and female submissiveness, thus abolishing patriarchal authority, and to replace it with the concept of equal rights for both sexes. To practise the principle of equal pay for equal work, and to practise birth control

4 To eliminate the theory of women's backwardness, attacking it with the idea of women as 'half of heaven'

5 To eliminate the attitudes of 'studying to make yourself somebody' and 'going to work on the land so that you will be well thought of' – opposing them with the ideas that 'studying serves the people' and that agricultural labour must be given its proper value.

The women of Yuan Ping Street organized a campaign centred on these 'five destructions and five reconstructions'. They gave some indication of the extent of their mobilization in the course of a few weeks. They held study sessions, criticism meetings, assemblies and debates. They edited newspapers, wrote articles in the press and on *dazibaos* (wall posters written in large characters). A total of 1200 women from Yuan Ping Street played an active part in this campaign. Extra evening classes in political study had to be organized, since the number of women attending doubled, and in those classes women who had felt too insignificant to talk in public before at last dared to speak out.

Other newspaper articles record the fact that the offensive against male chauvinism is being carried out simultaneously on three fronts.

Firstly, the real activities of women are publicized, thus demonstrating how times have changed. The achievements of women for their communities in one area or another are now written up on wall posters. One such poster comes from Yuan Ping:

Following the appeal of the May 7 directive, the women in the district undertook to prepare new fields for planting. They have prepared them. For three consecutive years they have harvested a crop yielding 75 quintals per hectare. Relying on their own strength, they have built small factories, and in that way have considerably increased industrial production. They have transformed the district from an area of 'consumption' to an area of 'production'. These undeniable facts constitute an irreversible refutation of the doctrine of contempt for women put forward by Confucius, Liu Shao-chi, Lin Piao and others.

Women will often affirm their membership of vanguard women's units across the country. National newspaper articles glorifying their exploits are commented on, studied and pasted up locally.

Secondly, there is a simultaneous denunciation of the Confucian doctrines according to which 'women are created to serve' and are 'difficult to manage'. 'women and children must have rules of conduct to keep them on the straight and narrow'; 'a woman belongs to her husband as a hen belongs to the rooster'; and 'the greatest happiness comes with the largest number of sons'.

The *People's Daily* editorial of 8 March 1974 is specific on this point: 'The theory of male supremacy and the theory of female slavery and dependence must both be mercilessly condemned and their sinister influence must be eliminated. Not only women but *men as well* must criticize these theories.'

Most of the time these criticisms are made by means of the example of actual cases known throughout a given locality. One such example tells how Hsieh Siou-yin had four daughters. She kept trying for a son to carry the family name and therefore refused to practise contraception. Another woman refused to become a cadre because she was afraid of not being equal to the task. Yet another didn't dare go out to work because she considered that her fate was to stay at home. Such examples are remnants of Confucianism and are not uncommon. Cases are studied by the local Women's Federation. All the women help to find a collective solution, and every success is publicized to encourage the others.

Thirdly, and finally, concrete steps are being taken for the long term. In particular small workshops are being set up. I recently visited an old quarter of Peking where the housewives still stayed at home. For the most part they were fairly elderly women, retired workers or women who were handicapped or in delicate health. It was impossible in practice for these women to participate in the work of the neighbouring small factories. The residents' committee, having studied the problem, set up a small factory (a May 7 workshop) [16] to manufacture theatrical props like paper flowers or garlands. The workshop, situated right in the centre of a network of small streets, makes it possible for women to work when they can and for as long as they can. They organize the production themselves and they get a wage for work which is not only useful and necessary to the State, but which also enables them to meet together and to break through the isolation that they would otherwise suffer.

A critique of the three obediences and the four virtues has recently emerged. The three obediences were preached by Mencius and Confucius and demanded that a woman should obey her father and her elder brothers before marriage, her husband during marriage and her sons when widowed. The four virtues rigidly determined a woman's public behaviour – her conduct, conversational subjects, dress and domestic tasks. A woman was obliged to be moderate in all circumstances and to observe the proper attitudes in her speech and her conduct. Her conversation was to be demure and restrained, so as not to bore men. When laughing she was obliged to cover her mouth, because it was considered immodest to show her teeth and tongue. Her choice of dress was dictated by the single need to please men. Last but not least, she had to fulfil all her domestic chores with good grace.

'Away with this decadent ideology!' can be heard and read everywhere – even though you won't find many people in China today [17] openly defending the literal interpretation of these feudal rules.

But as I said at the beginning of this article, these ideas are still influencing people at every turn. Confucian doctrine has weighed the Chinese masses down for 2500 years and they still bear its marks. It is an extremely élitist doctrine, almost racist in its treatment of the people, and of women in particular. *Today*, the Chinese bourgeoisie *still* relies on Confucianism for its counter-revolutionary projects and the current anti-Confucian movement is, therefore, of crucial importance to the future of the Chinese revolution. Radically to discredit Confucianism among the masses is to deal a crippling blow to reaction. But this is no mean task and will involve a protracted struggle. In fact this struggle has not ceased in the whole fifty years of the life of the Chinese Communist Party. The difference is that this time the assault is planned and thoroughgoing.

Women are at the heart of the struggle. All the patriarchal relations inherited from feudalism are disrupted when age-old submissiveness is rejected. Solidarity comes to life among those women who struggle against the 'total power' of husbands, who fight against respect for the authority of educationalists, and who reject the religion of material incentives. The most important ideological themes of the struggle have profound consequences for women. Take, for instance, the radical critique of genius. Apart from the fact that 'geniuses' everywhere are usually men, the very idea of genius, of an innate and overwhelming predisposition for certain tasks at the expense of others, is at the root of *all theoretical systems* supporting discrimination against women. It is, therefore, understandable that women have much to say and much to gain from denouncing the idea of genius. Or take another example: the attack on contempt for manual work and for the governed masses. It is inconceivable that this attack could succeed unless the female masses, oppressed manual workers since time immemorial, by the dictate of ancient practice, fuse their experience with the ongoing revolution.

The 'Pi Lin Pi Kong' campaign is another means by which the people learn to delve below the surface in their attempts to reach and understand the fundamental nature of phenomena. 'It is essential to criticize the feudal thinking of looking down on women ... They were the most oppressed among the oppressed people. Such economic and political status of women gave rise to their strong desire for the revolution ... and they are imbued with *extremely great enthusiasm for socialism.'* [18] Seeing only the superficial inferiority of women is not just an illustory vision, but will in practice deprive the revolution of *its greatest enthusiasts.*

The 8 March 1973 editorial of the *People's Daily* denounced those who believed that women wouldn't be able to play a significant part in the 'Pi Lin Pi Kong' campaign because of their low cultural standards. These people would really like the campaign to remain no more than a mere academic exercise, an intellectual debate on the finer points of ancient history. As the struggle develops it will become obvious that women, far from being backward, are actually a vital motive force behind the 'Pi Lin Pi Kong' campaign.

Once again the Chinese revolution reminds us of the central role played by the class struggle. To deny that women are still disciminated against, to settle for legalistic verbiage, in other words to suggest casually that women's liberation has finally been victorious is to run counter to the movement of history and to impede the struggle of women for their emancipation. It is to oppose Mao Tse-tung, who has explicitly and constantly reaffirmed that the emancipation of women demands a protracted and continuous struggle. 'Only in the course of the socialist transformation of society can women gradually liberate themselves.' Until this transformation is complete, the liberation of women will be partial and still susceptible to a defeat that would return women to their earlier oppression.

Chinese women today have *profoundly improved* their position. That's the crucial point from which all their contemporary struggles start. Denying this change or underestimating it; limiting your vision to the surface of the matter or taking a few facts in isolation; refusing to see the *overall direction* of the revolution means, like it or not, adopting the viewpoint of a dead metaphysic. And to do that is to align yourself with the Chinese tendency that denies 'socialist innovations' and the gains of the Cultural Revolution.

This tendency has two phases. First of all there is the effort to impede or distort the changes brought about by the Cultural Revolution (the educational reforms, for example). Then, confronted by the temporary difficulties so created, there is the disingenuous exclamation: 'The Cultural Revolution has changed nothing and has served no purpose. What a waste, what a mess!' Women suffer the same indignities. The tendency opposes their initiatives as it opposes the revolution. Measures helping women are thwarted or sabotaged, and then comes the cry, 'Women are worried about nothing but their own little families. That's part of their nature and nothing can be done about it.' But Chinese women have risen against this tendency. Once more they confront reactionaries and reactionary nostalgia. Yet again they attack the eternal woman. One thing you can be sure of – this time won't be the last.

Notes and References

PART ONE

Introduction

1 See *Chine nouvelle*, LXI (March 1968), p. 8, 'Chinese women reject the revisionist line in the women's movement'.

Chapter 1

1 The Peking local government was a stronghold of Liu Shao-chi's partisans. It would frequently intervene in the management of factories to enforce a policy of 'rationalization' of work, as here. It was trying to reduce workers' control.
2 Tachai, a famous Chinese people's commune, was cited by Mao Tse-tung as an example of the way to build socialism in the Chinese countryside.
3 *Red Flag (Hongqi)* is the official organ of the Central Committee of the Chinese Communist Party.
4 Cited in *La Nouvelle Chine*, VIII (1972).
5 The distribution of revenue is done annually after the autumn harvest, taking the production team (unit of farm production) as the basis for calculation. Every month each team member gives himself or herself the points he (or she) thinks he has earned for his own work; this is done in collective discussion, during which comrades intervene if they disagree with his self-evaluation, whether they consider it too low or too high. The allocation of work points for women was the immediate cause of the controversy.

Chapter 2

1 Brigades are the agricultural production units. Several brigades make up a people's commune. Most brigades were formed by the reorganization of an already existing village community.
2 May 7 cadre schools were set up during the Cultural Revolution. Their purpose is to re-educate cadres in industry, commerce and administration.

PART TWO

Introduction

1 F. Engels, *The Origin of the Family, Private Property and the State*, in K. Marx and F. Engels, *Selected Works* (London, Lawrence & Wishart, 1968), pp. 509–10.
2 Christiane Collange, *Madame et le management*. p. 72.

Chapter 3

1 A. Kollontai, *Communism and the family* (London, Pluto Press, 1972), pp. 12–13.
2 Cited in H. K. Geiger, *The Family in Soviet Russia* (Cambridge, Mass.: Harvard University Press, 1968), p. 79.
3 *Peking Review* (24 September 1971), pp. 11–14; emphasis emphasis added.
4 *Weekday schedule to be followed by adult-workers, as seen by Kuzmin.*

1	lights out		22.00
2	eight hours' of sleep. Reveille		6.00
3	calisthenics	5 minutes	6.05
4	toilet	10 minutes	6.15
5	shower (optional)	5 minutes	6.20
6	dress	5 minutes	6.25
7	to the dining-room	3 minutes	6.28
8	breakfast	15 minutes	6.43
9	to the cloakroom	2 minutes	6.45
10	put on outdoor clothing	5 minutes	6.50
11	to the mine	10 minutes	7.00
12	work in the mine	8 hours	15.00
13	to the commune	10 minutes	15.10
14	take off outdoor clothing	7 minutes	15.17
15	wash	8 minutes	15.25
16	dinner	30 minutes	15.55
17	to rest-room for free hour	3 minutes	15.58
18	free hour. Those who wish may nap.	1 hour	16.58
19	toilet and change clothes	10 minutes	17.08
20	to the dining-room	2 minutes	17.10
21	tea	15 minutes	17.25

(Cited in A. Kopp, *Town and Revolution* [London, Thames & Hudson, 1970], p. 153).
5 The translators have been unable to find the source of this quotation. However, the position is expressed in this extract from a Sabsovich pamphlet:

The individual household must be replaced by communal establishments catering for the primary needs of the workers. Vast factory-like kitchens, in numbers sufficient to serve the entire population, must completely supersede home cooking. This will considerably improve the nation's feeding while greatly cheapening it. A corresponding apparatus, sufficiently complex and mechanized, must be created not only for preparing food, but to provide a more convenient way of feeding the population: an organization of large communal dining-halls at centres of work and in rest centres, in the creches, in social and educational institutions, etc.; a large-scale extension and perfection of the canning industries, etc.; in many cases the most convenient and expedient way of obtaining ready-made food at home will be this mechanised method. *The U.S.S.R. after another 15 years,* cited in R. Schlesinger, *The Family in the U.S.S.R.* (London, Routledge & Kegan Paul, 1949), p. 170].

6 Kopp, *op. cit.,* p. 155.
7 Yvon, *'L'U.R.S.S. telle qu'elle est.* ed. lPes d'or.
8 William Hinton, *Fanshen – A Documentary of Revolution in a Chinese Village* (Harmondsworth, Penguin, 1972).

Chapter 4

1 See Anna Louise Strong, *Letter from China,* XLIV-XLV (15 December 1967).
2 *Ibid.*

Chapter 5

1 'Les Communistes et la condition de la femme' (1970), a study carried out among women

by the Central Committee of Labour of the Communist Party; emphasis added.
2 Clara Zetkin, *My recollections of Lenin* (Moscow, 1956).
3 'Les Communistes et la condition de la femme', p. 44.
4 *Ibid.*, p. 47.
5 PCF (Party Programme). *Changer de cap* (Paris, Editions Sociales, 1971), p. 66; emphasis added.

PART THREE

Chapter 6

1 Cited in H. Geiger, *The Family in Soviet Russia* (Cambridge, Mass.: Harvard University Press, 1968), p. 72.
2 Cited in Schlesinger, *op. cit.*, p. 54.
3 Kate Millett, *Sexual Politics* (London, Sphere 1972), pp. 126–7; emphasis added.

Chapter 7

1 *La morale au cours élémentaire, Classiques Hachette* (Paris, Hachette, 1966).
2 C. Baudelot and R. Establet, *L'Ecole capitaliste en France* (Paris, Maspéro 1971).
3 The members of such groups are chosen according to the following political criteria: they must have had shop-floor experience; they must be involved in the class struggle, especially in the struggle against revisionism; they must practise socialist principles at work; they must be able to lead the ideological struggle to unite the masses around revolutionary positions, and especially to fight against sectarianism and divisive splitting; they must apply themselves to the study of Marxism, Leninism and Mao Tse-tung's thought. The teams are directed by the Communist Party, but not all workers are party members.
4 Cited in Volpicelli, *L'éducation en URSS*, p. 209; emphasis added.
5 Cited in Schlesinger, *op. cit.;* pp. 363–4emphasis added.
6 Cited in Volpicelli, *op. cit.*, p. 209; emphasis added.
7 It's not only in secondary schools that boys and girls learn to sew. We saw little boys of three or four in a Shanghai kindergarten sewing buttons on jackets.

Chapter 8

1 Cited in Geiger, *op. cit.*, pp. 47–8.

PART FOUR

Chapter 9

1 Lu Hsun, *Chinese Literature*, IX (1971).
2 Cited in Roxane Witke, 'Mao Tse tung, Women and Suicide', in *Women in China* ed. Marilyn B. Young, *Michigan Papers in Chinese Studies* (Ann Arbor, University of Michigan Press, 1973), pp. 16–17.
3 'A *k'ang* is a raised platform of mud bricks that usually takes up one whole side of a room in a Chinese house. It is so constructed that the flue from the cooking fire runs under it and warms it. In the winter the women live and work on the *k'ang* during the day' (Hinton, *op. cit.*, pp. 42–3n).
4 Hinton, *op. cit.*, pp. 185–6.
5 F. Engels, *Origin of the Family, Private Property and State*, in Marx and Engels, *op. cit.*, p. 512.
6 *Ibid.*
7 Teng Ying-chao, *The Marriage Law of the People's Republic of China* (Peking, Foreign Language Press 1950), pp. 38–40.
8 So as to remove any possible confusion, Teng Ying-chao stresses this point in the same ar-

ticle: 'The only way to eliminate the various chaotic phenomena in marriage in the transitional period is to carry out the Marriage Law in its entirety, to *completely abolish the feudal marriage system* and to establish the New Democratic marriage system. It is also necessary to educate the people on a long-term basis and *to promote new social morals*' (p. 34).

Chapter 10

1 See F. Engels, *Anti-Duhring* (Moscow, Progress Publishers, 1954), p. 385, for this example and a discussion of this point.
2 Christine Dupont, 'Libération des femmes, année zéro', in *Partisans*, LIV-V (1970).
3 See K. Marx, *Economic and Philosophic Manuscripts of 1844* (New York, International Publishers, 1964), pp. 72–3:
   ... In his work therefore, he [the worker] does not affirm himself but denies himself, does not feel content but unhappy, does not develop freely his physical and mental energy but mortifies his body and ruins his mind. The worker therefore only feels himself outside his work, and in his work feels outside himself. He is at home when he is not working, and when he is working he is not at home. His labour is therefore not voluntary, but coerced; it is *forced labour*. It is therefore not the satisfaction of a need; it is merely a *means* to satisfy needs external to it. Its alien character emerges clearly in the fact that as soon as no physical or other compulsion exists, labour is shunned like the plague ... As a result, therefore, man [the worker] only feels himself freely active in his animal functions – eating, drinking, procreating, or at most in his dwelling and in dressing-up, etc.; and in his human functions he no longer feels himself to be anything but an animal. What is animal becomes human and what is human becomes animal.
4 On this topic see J.-M. Konczyk, *Gaston, l'aventure d'un ouvrier, bit le Coeur ed.*
5 V. I. Lenin, 'International Women's day, March 8, 1921', in *Collected Works* (London, Lawrence & Wishart, 1961), XXXII.

Chapter 11

1 '... the children have the duty to support and to assist their parents', Teng Ying-chao, *op. cit.*, ch. 14, article 13.
2 *Ibid.*

PART FIVE

Chapter 12

1 K. Marx, *Critique of Political Economy* (London, Lawrence & Wishart, 1971), p. 197.
2 Lenin, *Collected Works*, XXXV, p. 183.
3 The degradation of sexuality is rooted mainly in the fact that sexual life is divorced from all other areas of social life and is relegated to the rank of activities devoid of awareness. Marx noted: 'Certainly eating, drinking, procreating, etc., are also genuinely human functions. But abstractly taken, separated from the sphere of all other human activity and turned into sole and ultimate ends, they are animal functions' (*Economic and Philosophic Manuscripts*, p. 111).

Chapter 13

1 Geiger, *op. cit.*, chs III and IV.
2 *La Nouvelle Chine*, II, p. 31.
3 'Sortir de l'ombre', a discussion paper by the Dimitriev group of the French Women's Liberation Movement, published as a supplement to *Le Torchon Brûle* (a French femininist newspaper).
4 *La Nouvelle Chine*, I, p. 39.

Chapter 14

1 Teng Ying-chao, *op. cit.*, p. 40.

Afterword

1 This is the complete text of an article written by the author in 1973 and published in the French periodical *Chine 74* (April, 1974).
2 The *People's Daily (Renmin Ribao)* is the official newspaper of the Chinese government.
3 'Pi Lin Pi Kong' – an abbreviation used in China to denote the campaign of criticism waged against Confucius and Lin Piao.
4 *Red Flag*, XII (1 December, 1973).
5 The women workers in the Chao Yan factory in Peking that I had visited in 1971 and returned to in 1973 told me that during the Cultural Revolution four out of the six qualified young women in the kindergarten left their jobs because they thought the work 'too inglorious', and not noble enough. It was, at that time, impossible to convince them that the people could be served in places other than the factories. It's easy to imagine the repercussions their attitude could have had on the functioning of the crèches, and therefore on the liberation of women.
6 It's worth mentioning in this connection an important article in the March 1974 issue of *China Reconstructs*, 'How we women won equality', in which the author, Tsui Yu-lan, smashes this 'theory'.
7 I have noticed a net growth in the proportion of women in positions of leadership and in other areas such as higher education, since the visit to China which led to the writing of this book. In 1971 we were told that the Party's aim was to have 30 per cent women in the various positions of leadership. Today many people say that this is only one phase and that 30 per cent represents a figure that must be quickly exceeded. The revolutionary committee of Tsinghua University gave us the following figures for the proportion of women in the student population: 27 per cent in 1971, 30 per cent in 1972 and 34 per cent in 1973. The chairman of the committee added, 'This progress is encouraging but we can't be pleased with these figures. We must quickly reach 50 per cent, really half of heaven.'
This example is particularly interesting when you realize that Tsinghua is a scientific and technical university specializing in areas which have been traditionally masculine.
8 The press is full of reports and tables – not to mention critical articles like the one in *Red Flag* – describing people's communes, districts and factories where these reforms have been implemented and telling of the progress women there have made towards actually becoming 'half of heaven'.
9 Domestic-service workshops (laundries, clothes manufacture and repair workshops, cleaners and so on), canteens, health centres, crèches and kindergartens attached to various productive or housing units are all described by the term 'social public welfare facilities'.
10 The author of this article could be making a veiled reference to difficulties which have actually hindered the efficient provision of pre-school care. The Peking teacher-training school for kindergarten teachers has been closed since 1966 and, to the best of my knowledge, is still closed. It has produced no newly qualified teachers for at least eight years. 'This is one way in which right-wing policies have shown themselves,' we were told in Peking's No. 5 Kindergarten. Such interference from the right has posed, and no doubt still poses, serious problems. The network of crèches and kindergartens needs to be extended at a time when the source of newly qualified teachers has dried up. Moreover, there are regulations specifying a certain ratio of qualified staff in crèches. Observing the regulation is often equivalent to refusing a new intake of children. This was especially true three or four years after the Cultural Revolution, which saw an increase in the birthrate. Faced with this situation, some crèches (especially those run directly by factory or district committees) ignore the regulations and recruit their staff directly from among women factory workers or housewives of the district – the crèche in the No. 3 textile factory in Peking has two qualified women out of a staff of forty; at Chao Yan, two out of twenty are qualified.

However, it seems that crèches run by various administrative bodies, further education establishments or even the State, suffer from this state of affairs.

11 'Report from a production brigade in Kiangsu', *Red Flag* (March 1973).

12 On our visit to the Sino-Cuban people's commune, near Peking, the leader of the commune recounted its experiences in this area – difficulties as well as successes. He concluded: 'The main tasks of the women's committee are 1) to carry out ideological work among women; 2) to speak for all women and to defend them in their family or elsewhere; and 3) to be responsible for women's work. For instance, women can't do exactly the same work as men during their periods. Yet because feudal ideas still persist women don't want to talk about their periods. The women's committee, which knows the women well and knows the dates of their periods, can speak for them. The women's committee also intervenes if *the equal pay principle isn't correctly applied* – which does happen. Without a women's committee, there is no guarantee of women's equal rights.

13 Yang Po-lan and Chen Pei-chen, Hsinhua News Agency (22 February 1974).

14 I shall just mention here the example of the problem of housework, which I have already discussed at length.

15 In reading these five points the reader must, of course, bear in mind that they refer to a *continuous* process of *radical* change, started at the very inception of the Chinese revolution.

16 The May 7 workshops, created after Chairman Mao's directive of the same name, have a different function from that of the small street factories. Their main task seems to be to organize collective productive labour for people who are either too old or too weak to cope with factory schedules and work. The internal division of labour in these workshops is loosely defined , so that one person's absence, for example, doesn't upset the work of others. They are usually subcontracted by small street factories or state factories to produce parts. Not only does such a system of production meet the real needs of society but, and this is perhaps most important, the collective set-up immediately allows women working there to take charge of the workshop and to organize political and cultural study groups so that they, too, can participate in the socialist reconstruction (see also the article on women tackling this question in *Peking Information*, XII [1973]).

17 I mean of course mainland China. Under Nationalist rule the non-liberated part of China still sees Confucian doctrine as the infallible and rigid governing code for the people.

18 *Red Flag* (December 1973).